CULTURAL STUDIES
AND THE STUDY OF
POPULAR CULTURE:
THEORIES AND METHODS

CULTURAL STUDIES AND THE STUDY OF POPULAR CULTURE: THEORIES AND METHODS

John Storey

University of Georgia Press
Athens

for Kate and Jenny
and to the memory of my mother and father

Published in the United States of
America in 1996 by
The University of Georgia Press,
Athens, Georgia 30602

© 1996 by John Storey
All rights reserved

First published in Great Britain in
1996 by Edinburgh University Press

Typeset in Linotype Sabon by
Hewer Text Composition Services,
Edinburgh, and
printed and bound in Great Britain

ISBN 0 8203 1869 8 (pbk.)

Library of Congress Cataloguing
in Publication Data is available
upon request.

Contents

Acknowledgements

I would like to take this opportunity to thank all those who have contributed, knowingly and unknowingly, to the writing of this book, especially family, friends, colleagues and students (past and present). I would also like to thank the School of Arts, Design and Communications, University of Sunderland, for lightening my teaching load during the course of writing this book. Finally, I would especially like to thank Paul Marris, Jackie Jones, Jannette Storey, Jenny Storey, Kate Storey, and Sue Thornham, for their support and encouragement throughout.

1

CULTURAL STUDIES AND THE STUDY OF POPULAR CULTURE: AN INTRODUCTION

The aim of this book is twofold: first, to introduce students and other interested readers to the study of contemporary popular culture; and second, to suggest a map of the development of cultural studies through a discussion of a range of theories and methods for the study of popular culture. I have not attempted an elaborate mapping of the field. Rather, my aim has been to bring together under discussion a range of approaches which have made a significant contribution to the development of the cultural studies approach to the study of contemporary popular culture. It is hoped the book will provide a useful introduction – and range of *usable* theories and methods – for students new to the field, and a critical overview for those more familiar with the procedures and politics of cultural studies.[1]

CULTURAL STUDIES AND POPULAR CULTURE

Cultural studies is not a monolithic body of theories and methods. Stuart Hall (1992) makes this very clear:

> Cultural Studies has multiple discourses; it has a number of different histories. It is a whole set of formations; it has its own different conjunctures and moments in the past. It included many different kinds of work ... It always was a set of unstable formations ... It had many trajectories; many

1

> people had and have different theoretical positions, all of them in contention. (278)

Cultural studies has always been an unfolding discourse, responding to changing historical and political conditions and always marked by debate, disagreement and intervention. For example, in the late 1970s the centrality of class in cultural studies was disrupted first by feminism's insistence on the importance of gender, and then by black students raising questions about the invisibility of race in much cultural studies analysis. It is simply not possible *now* to think of cultural studies and popular culture, for example, without also thinking about the enormous contribution to the study of popular culture made by feminism. In the early 1970s, such a connection would have been far from obvious.

Although it is misleading – and probably not desirable – to limit cultural studies to an academic orthodoxy, it is possible to present, for the purposes of an introduction, some of its basic assumptions.

'Culture' in cultural studies is defined politically rather than aesthetically. The object of study in cultural studies is not culture defined in the narrow sense, as the objects of aesthetic excellence ('high art'); nor culture defined in an equally narrow sense, as a process of aesthetic, intellectual and spiritual development; but culture understood as the texts and practices of everyday life. This is a definition of culture which can embrace the first two definitions; but also, and crucially, it can range beyond the social exclusivity and narrowness of these, to include the study of popular culture. Although cultural studies cannot (and should not) be reduced to the study of popular culture, it is certainly the case that the study of popular culture is central to the project of cultural studies.

Cultural studies also regards culture as political in a quite specific sense – as a terrain of conflict and contestation. It is seen as a key site for the production and reproduction of the social relations of everyday life. Perhaps the best-known elaboration of this way of seeing culture comes from Stuart Hall (in Storey 1994). He describes popular culture, for example, as

> an arena of consent and resistance. It is partly where hegemony arises, and where it is secured. It is not a sphere where

2

socialism, a socialist culture – already fully formed – might be simply 'expressed'. But it is one of the places where socialism might be constituted. That is why 'popular culture' matters. (466)

Others within cultural studies might not express their attitude to popular culture quite in these terms, but they would certainly share Hall's concern to think culture politically.

Cultural studies is grounded in Marxism. Marxism informs cultural studies in two fundamental ways. First, to understand the meaning(s) of a cultural text or practice, we must analyse it in its social and historical conditions of production and consumption. However, although constituted by a particular social structure with a particular history, culture is not studied as a reflection of this structure and history. History and culture are not separate entities. It is never a question of reading a text or practice against its historical background or using a text or practice to illustrate an already formulated account of an historical moment – history and text/practice are inscribed in each other and are embedded together as a part of the same process. Cultural studies insists that culture's importance derives from the fact that it helps constitute the structure and shape the history. As Hall (in Storey 1996) explains,

> what cultural studies has helped me to understand is that the media [for example] play a part in the formation, in the constitution, of the things that they reflect. It is not that there is a world outside, 'out there', which exists free of the discourses of representation. What is 'out there' is, in part, constituted by how it is represented.

In other words, cultural texts, for example, do not simply reflect history, they make history and are part of its processes and practices and should, therefore, be studied for the (ideological) work that they do, rather than for the (ideological) work (always happening elsewhere) that they reflect.

The second assumption taken from Marxism is the recognition

that capitalist industrial societies are societies divided unequally along, for example, ethnic, gender, generational and class lines. Cultural studies contends that culture is one of the principal sites where this division is established and contested: culture is a terrain on which there takes place a continual struggle over meaning, in which subordinate groups attempt to resist the imposition of meanings which bear the interests of dominant groups. It is this which makes culture ideological.

Ideology is without doubt the central concept in cultural studies. There are a number of competing definitions of ideology, but it is the formulation established by Hall (1985) which is generally accepted as the dominant definition within cultural studies. Working within a framework of Antonio Gramsci's (1971: see Storey 1993) concept of 'hegemony', Hall developed a theory of 'articulation' to explain the processes of ideological struggle (Hall's use of 'articulation' plays on the term's double meaning: to express and to join together). He argues that cultural texts and practices are not inscribed with meaning, guaranteed once and for all by the intentions of production; meaning is always the result of an act of 'articulation' (an active process of 'production in use'). The process is called 'articulation' because meaning has to be expressed, but it is always expressed in a specific context, a specific historical moment, within a specific discourse(s). Thus expression is always connected to and conditioned by context. Hall also draws on the work of the Russian theorist Valentin Volosinov (1973). Volosinov argues that meaning is always determined by context of articulation. Cultural texts and practices are 'multiaccentual'; that is, they can be articulated with different 'accents' by different people in different contexts for different politics. Meaning is therefore a social production; the world has to be made to mean. A text or practice or event is not the issuing source of meaning, but a site where the articulation of meaning – variable meaning(s) – can take place. And because different meanings can be ascribed to the same text or practice or event, meaning is always a potential site of conflict. Thus the field of culture is for cultural studies a major site of ideological struggle; a terrain of 'incorporation' and 'resistance'; one of the sites where hegemony is to be won or lost.

In response to the dual challenge represented by the undermining of the Marxist paradigm, both by the events in Eastern Europe and the attacks of postmodern critics (see McRobbie 1992, 1994 and Storey 1996), many in cultural studies have begun to rethink its political project. Angela McRobbie's (1994) response to the 'crisis' in cultural studies is to argue for a return to neo-Gramscian hegemony theory. She accepts that cultural studies has been radically transformed as debates about postmodernism and postmodernity have replaced the more familiar debates about ideology and hegemony. Cultural studies, she claims, has responded in two ways. On the one hand, it has prompted a return to economic reductive forms of analysis; and on the other, it has given rise to an uncritical celebration of consumerism, in which consumption is understood *too* exclusively in terms of pleasure and meaning-making. McRobbie rejects a return 'to a crude and mechanical base-superstructure model, and also the dangers of pursuing a kind of cultural populism to a point at which anything which is consumed and is popular is also seen as oppositional' (39). Instead, she calls for 'an extension of Gramscian cultural analysis' (39), and for a return to ethnographic cultural analysis which takes as its object of study '[t]he lived experience which breathes life into [the] . . . inanimate objects [of popular culture]' (27).

The cultural studies use of hegemony theory – what Hall (1992) calls 'the enormously productive metaphor of hegemony' (280) – at its best insists that there is a dialectic between the processes of production and the activities of consumption. The consumer always confronts a text or practice in its material existence as a result of determinate conditions of production. But in the same way, the text or practice is confronted by a consumer who in effect *produces in use* the range of possible meaning(s), which cannot just be read off from the materiality of the text or practice, or the means or relations of its production.

Cultural studies would also insist that making popular culture ('production in use') can be empowering to subordinate and resistant to dominant understandings of the world. But this is not to say that popular culture is always empowering and resistant. To deny the passivity of consumption is not to deny that sometimes consumption is passive; to deny that the consumers of popular culture are not cultural dupes is not to deny that at times we can all be duped. But it is to deny that popular culture is little more than a degraded culture, successfully imposed from above, to make profit and secure ideological control. The best of cultural studies insists that to decide these matters requires vigilance and attention to the details of the production, distribution and consumption of culture. These are not matters that can be decided once and for all (outside the contingencies of history and politics) with an elitist glance and a condescending sneer. Nor can they be read off from the moment of production (locating meaning, pleasure, ideological effect, etc. in, variously, the intention, the means of production or the production itself): these are only aspects of the contexts for 'production in use', and it is, ultimately, in 'production in use' that questions of meaning, pleasure, ideological effect, etc. can be (contingently) decided. Moreover, it is important to distinguish between the power of the culture industries and the power of their influence. Too often the two are conflated, but they are not necessarily the same.

Let me conclude these introductory remarks with a long, but rewarding, quotation from the American cultural studies theorist Lawrence Grossberg (1992b). In so many ways, it sums up what I have been trying to say.

> We have to acknowledge that, for the most part, the relationship between the audience and popular texts is an active and productive one. The meaning of a text is not given in some independently available set of codes which we can consult at our own convenience. A text does not carry its own meaning or politics already inside of itself; no text is able to guarantee what its effects will be. People are constantly struggling, not merely to figure out what a text means, but to make it mean something that connects to their own lives, experiences, needs and desires. The same text will mean different things to different people, depending on how it is interpreted. And different people have different interpretive resources, just as they have different needs. A text can only mean something in the context of the experience and situation of its particular

6

audience. Equally important, texts do not define ahead of time how they are to be used or what functions they can serve. They can have different uses for different people in different contexts . . . How a specific text is used, how it is interpreted, how it functions for its audience – all of these are inseparably connected through the audience's constant struggle to make sense of itself and its world, even more, to make a slightly better place for itself in the world. (52–3)

MORE ABOUT THIS BOOK

My aim, as stated earlier, is to present a range of theories and methods which have been used within cultural studies to study contemporary popular culture. In the main, I have tried to keep criticisms of the theories and methods to a minimum. I have, therefore, tried to avoid 'opinion writing', where, instead of explaining a theory or method, the author continually clutters his or her account with talk of problems and how he or she would solve them or would do the whole thing differently. There is of course a place for such an approach, but I am not convinced that the appropriate place is an introductory text. I would like the reader to take from this book an understanding of a range of significant theories and methods, rather than an understanding of what I think about them. Now it may, at times, become obvious what I think, but this should not be the primary knowledge that the reader takes from the book. For much the same reasons, I have quoted more than would be appropriate in a more 'advanced' text. But I feel quite strongly that introductory texts work best when they give their readers reasonable access to the theories and theorists under discussion.

I am also aware that I have simplified the field. Selection always means exclusion; and I know that my selection will not meet with universal approval. There are other valuable theories and methods which I have not discussed. In my defence, I can say only that it is not possible in a book of this size to cover all the theories and methods which have influenced cultural studies or which form part of its very structure. I have, however, selected the approaches which *I* believe are most significant.

In conclusion, it is difficult to do full justice to the complexities of the theories and methods that I have discussed. To really do justice to the range and diversity of the study of contemporary popular culture within cultural studies would be the work of more than one book. Finally, whatever else this book is, it is certainly not intended as a substitute for reading first-hand the theories and methods discussed.

NOTES

1. For a fuller version of this history, with particular reference to popular culture, see Storey 1993, 1994 and 1996.

2

TELEVISION

Television is *the* popular cultural form of the late twentieth century.
It is without doubt the world's most popular leisure activity. On the
day you are reading this book, there will be around the world in
excess of 3.5 billion hours spent watching[1] television (Kubey and
Csikszentmihalyi 1990: 1). British audiences, for example, spend
on average more than one-third of their waking hours watching
television. In the USA, average time spent viewing is about twice as
much (Allen 1992: 13). The 'average' American will spend in excess
of seven years watching television (Kubey and Csikszentimhalyi
1990: xi).

ENCODING AND DECODING TELEVISUAL DISCOURSE

If we are in search of a founding moment when cultural studies
first emerges from left-Leavisism, 'pessimistic' versions of Marxism,
American mass communication models, culturalism and structuralism, the publication of Stuart Hall's 'Encoding and Decoding in the
Television Discourse' (Hall 1973) is perhaps it.[2]

In Hall's model of televisual communication (see Figure 1), the
circulation of 'meaning' in televisual discourse passes through three
distinctive moments: 'each has its specific modality and conditions
of existence' (128). First, media professionals put into meaningful

9

televisual discourse their particular account of, for example, a 'raw' social event. At this moment in the circuit, a range of ways of looking at the world ('ideologies') are 'in dominance'.

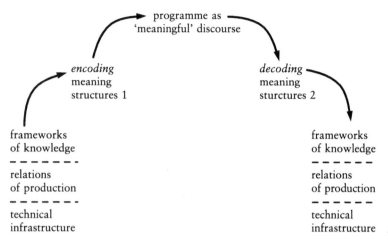

Figure I

> [The moment of media production] is framed throughout by meanings and ideas; knowledge-in-use concerning the routines of production, historically defined technical skills, professional ideologies, institutional knowledge, definitions and assumptions, assumptions about the audience and so on frame the constitution of the programme through this production structure. Further, though the production structures of television originate the television discourse, they do not constitute a closed system. They draw topics, treatments, agendas, events, personnel, images of the audience, 'definitions of the situation' from other sources and other discursive formations within the wider socio-cultural and political structure of which they are a differentiated part. (129)

Thus the media professionals involved determine how the 'raw' social event will be encoded in discourse. However, in the second moment, once the meanings and messages are in meaningful discourse, that is, once they have taken the form of televisual discourse, the formal rules of language and discourse are 'in dominance'; the message is now open, for example, to the play of polysemy.

> Since the visual discourse translates a three-dimensional world into two-dimensional planes, it cannot, of course, *be* the refer-ent or concept it signifies . . . Reality exists outside language, but it is constantly mediated by and through language: and what we can know and say has to be produced in and through discourse. Discursive 'knowledge' is the product not of the transparent representation of the 'real' in language but of the articulation of language on real relations and conditions. Thus there is no intelligible discourse without the operation of a code. (131)

Finally, in the third moment, the moment of audience decoding, another range of ways of looking at the world ('ideologies') are 'in dominance'. An audience is confronted not by a 'raw' social event, but by a discursive translation of the event. If the event is to become 'meaningful' to the audience, it must decode and make sense of the discourse. 'If no "meaning" is taken, there can be no "consumption"'. If the meaning is not articulated in practice, it has no effect' (128). If an audience acts upon its decoding, this then becomes itself a social practice, a 'raw' social event, available to be encoded in another discourse. Thus, through the circulation of discourse, 'production' becomes 'reproduction' to become 'production' again. The circuit starts in the 'social' and ends, to begin again, in the 'social'.

In other words, meanings and messages are not simply 'trans-mitted', they are always produced: first by the encoder from the 'raw' material of everyday life; second, by the audience in relation to its location in other discourses. Each moment is 'determinate', operating in its own conditions of production. Moreover, as Hall makes clear, the moments of encoding and decoding may not be perfectly symmetrical. There is nothing inevitable about the outcome of the process – what is intended and what is taken may not coincide. Media professionals may wish decoding to correspond with encoding, but they cannot prescribe or guarantee this. Governed by different conditions of existence, encoding and decoding are open to variable reciprocity. There is always the possibility of misunderstanding.

> No doubt misunderstandings of a literal kind do exist. The viewer does not know the terms employed, cannot follow the complex logic of argument or exposition, is unfamiliar with the language, finds the concepts too alien or difficult or is foxed by the expository narrative. But more often broadcasters are concerned that the audience has failed to take the meaning as they – the broadcasters – intended. What they really mean to say is that viewers are not operating within the 'dominant' or 'preferred' code. (135)

It is this second 'misunderstanding' which interests Hall. Drawing on the work of sociologist Frank Parkin (1971), he suggests 'three hypothetical positions from which decodings of a televisual discourse may be constructed' (136). The first position he calls 'the dominant-hegemonic position' (136). This occurs '[w]hen the viewer takes the connoted meaning from, say, a television newscast or current affairs programme full and straight, and decodes the message in terms of the reference code in which it has been encoded, we might say that the viewer *is operating inside the dominant code*' (136). To decode a television discourse in this way is to be in harmony with the 'professional code' of the broadcasters.

> The professional code is 'relatively independent' of the dominant code, in that it applies criteria and transformational operations of its own, especially those of a technico-practical nature. The professional code, however, operates *within* the 'hegemony' of the dominant code. Indeed, it serves to reproduce the dominant definitions precisely by bracketing their hegemonic quality and operating instead with displaced professional codings which foreground such apparently neutral-technical questions as visual quality, news and presentational values, televisual quality, 'professionalism' and so on. (136)

The dominant code is always articulated through the professional code. David Morley (1980) gives the example of the way in which *Nationwide* reported the release of Patrick Meehan in 1976.

> What is 'not relevant' as far as they are concerned is the whole political background to the case. Now that is not to say that this is a straightforwardly ideological decision to block out the political implications of the case. It's much more, in their terms, a communicative decision, as it appears to them; that is their notion of 'good television', to deal in that kind of 'personal drama'. (152)

The second decoding position is 'the negotiated code or position' (137). This is probably the majority position.

> Decoding within the negotiated version contains a mixture of adaptive and oppositional elements: it acknowledges the legitimacy of the hegemonic definitions to make the grand significations (abstract), while, at a more restricted, situational (situated) level, it makes its own ground rules – it operates with exceptions to the rule. It accords the privileged position to the dominant definitions of events while reserving the right to make a more negotiated application to 'local conditions', to its own *corporate* positions. This negotiated version of the dominant ideology is thus shot through with contradictions, though these are only on certain occasions brought to full visibility. (137)

An example of the negotiated code might be a worker who agrees in general terms with the news report's claim that increased wages cause inflation, while insisting on his or her right to strike for better pay and conditions.

Finally, the third position identified by Hall is 'the oppositional code'. This is the position occupied by the viewer who recognises the preferred code of the televisual discourse but who nonetheless chooses to decode within an alternative frame of reference. 'This is the case [for example] of the viewer who listens to a debate on the need to limit wages but "reads" every mention of the "national interest" as "class interest" ' (138).

Hall acknowledges that his hypothetical decoding positions 'need to be empirically tested and refined' (136). This in part is the project of David Morley's *The 'Nationwide' Audience* (1980) – to test Hall's model, to see how individual interpretations of televisual texts relate to socio-cultural background. Morley provides a useful summary (and clarification of) his own working understanding of Hall's encoding/decoding model as follows:

1. The production of a meaningful message in the TV discourse is always problematic 'work'. The same event can be encoded in more than one way. The study here is, then, of how and why certain production practices and structures tend to produce certain messages, which embody their meanings in certain recurring forms.

2. The message in social communication is always complex in structure and form. It always contains more than one potential 'reading'. Messages propose and prefer certain readings over others, but they can never become wholly closed around one reading. They remain polysemic.

3. The activity of 'getting meaning' from the message is also a problematic practice, however transparent and 'natural' it may seem. Messages encoded one way can always be read in a different way. (10)

Morley arranged for twenty-nine different groups to view two episodes (from 1976 and 1977) of the BBC's early-evening magazine/news programme *Nationwide*. The first programme was shown to eighteen groups, the second to eleven. Each group consisted of five to ten people. The groups were selected on the basis that they might be expected to differ in their decodings from 'dominant' to 'negotiated' to 'oppositional'.

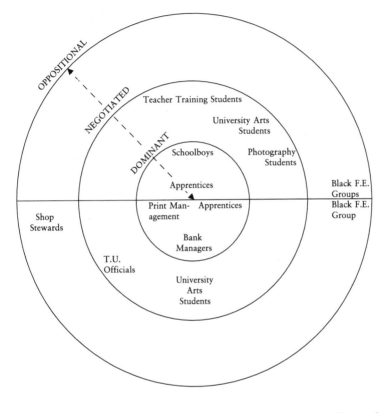

Figure 2

Morley analysed the different readings produced by each group. Much of what he found seemed to confirm Hall's model (see Figure 2 for Morley's diagrammatic presentation of his findings). For example, a group of university arts students and a group of teacher-training-college students produced readings which moved between 'negotiated' and 'dominant', while the group of shop stewards produced an 'oppositional reading'.[3] However, when the middle-class bank managers and the working-class apprentices both produced dominant readings, the correlation between class and reading position looked less secure, forcing Morley to acknowledge that decodings are not determined 'directly from social class position'. Rather, as he reformulates it: 'it is always a question of how social position *plus* particular discourse positions produce specific readings; readings which are structured because the structure of access to different discourses is determined by social position' (134).

In this way, Morley is able to explain the similarity in decodings between the working-class apprentices and the middle-class bank managers in terms of the formulation: determination of class plus other discourses (bodies of ideas and shared socio-cultural practices which help constitute us as social subjects and thus shape how we see and think about the world). Thus when we are interpellated by a text, this is always in a context of other interpellations. The text–reader encounter does not occur in a moment isolated from other discourses, but always in a field of many discourses, some in harmony with the text, some which are in contradiction with it. One reads, for example, as a student, a Catholic, a socialist and a member of a youth subculture. Each discourse may pull us in a different direction. Each may assume a different level of importance in any given social setting. The response of the black Further Education students and other predominantly black groups to *Nationwide* – their 'critique of silence' – is therefore not to be explained as a failure of communication (the technical inability of the encoders to get their message across). Rather, what it demonstrates is the discourses of the text coming into conflict with the discourses of the reader. 'Here', as Morley explains 'the action of the cultures and discourses which these groups are involved in acts to block or inflect their interpellation by the discourse of *Nationwide*' (143). The converse is also evident in the decodings made by the working-class apprentices. 'Here it is not simply a case of the absence of "contradictory" discourses; rather it is the presence of other discourses which work in parallel with those of the programme – enabling these groups to produce "corresponding" representations' (143). Other discourses are always in play, 'although their action is more visible when it is a case of negative-contradictory rather than positive-reinforcing effect' (144). As Morley explains:

[T]he social subject is always interpellated by a number of discourses, some of which are in parallel and reinforce each other, some of which are contradictory and block or inflect the successful interpellation of the subject by other discourses. Positively or negatively, other discourses are always involved in the relation of text and subject, although their action is simply more visible when it is a negative and contradictory rather than a positive and reinforcing effect. (162)

However, despite these other determinations (these other discourses), Morley still stresses the importance of class in that it determines access (or the nature of access) to different discourses. As he explains, 'the subject's position in the social formation structures his or her range of access to various discourses and ideological codes' (158). This then explains the correlation between the readings made by the bank managers and the apprentices. The bank managers produced a dominant reading because of their political commitment to the conservatism of *Nationwide's* discourse, while the apprentices accepted it uncritically because of a lack (unlike the shop stewards) of an alternative political discourse. Class was the key to both readings. The first was made on the basis of 'class interest', the second on the basis of the 'class interest' of the British education system (the working-class apprentices were schooled to be politically uncritical).

In the 'Afterword' to *The 'Nationwide' Audience*, Morley sums up (rather too modestly, in my opinion) the achievements of his research:

I have been able to do no more than to indicate some of the ways in which social position and (sub)cultural frameworks may be related to individual readings. To claim more than that, on the basis of such a small sample, would be misleading. Similarly, I would claim only to have shown the viability of an approach which treats the audience as a set of cultural groupings rather than as a mass of individuals or as a set of rigid socio-demographic categories. Clearly, more work needs to be done on the relation between group and individual readings. (163)

Regretting the absence from his research of any discussion of how the context of decoding might effect the decodings produced, Morley's next research (1986) was an exploration of television viewing in the family home.[4]

In the early 1980s, the Dutch cultural critic Ien Ang placed the following advertisement in *Viva*, a Dutch women's magazine: 'I like watching the TV serial *Dallas*, but often get odd reactions to it. Would anyone like to write and tell me why you like watching it too, or dislike it? I should like to assimilate these reactions in my university thesis. Please write to . . . (1985: 10).

The context for Ang's research was the emergence of the American 'prime-time soap' *Dallas* as an international success (watched in over ninety countries) in the early 1980s. In the Netherlands, *Dallas* was regularly watched by 52 per cent of the population.

Following the advertisement, Ang received forty-two letters (thirty-nine from women or girls) from both lovers and haters of *Dallas*. These form the empirical basis of her study of the pleasure(s) of watching *Dallas* for its predominantly female audience. She is not concerned with pleasure understood as the satisfaction of an already pre-existent need, but 'the mechanisms by which pleasure is aroused' (9). Instead of the question 'what are the effects of pleasure?' she poses the question 'what is the mechanism of pleasure; how is it produced and how does it work?'

For Ang's letter-writers the pleasure or displeasures of *Dallas* are inextricably linked with questions of 'realism'. The extent to which a letter-writer finds the programme 'good' or 'bad' is determined by whether they find it 'realistic' (good) or 'unrealistic' (bad). Critical of both 'empiricist realism' (a text is considered realistic to the extent it adequately reflects that which exists outside itself) and 'classic realism' (Colin McCabe's (1974) claim that realism is an illusion created by the extent to which a text can successfully conceal its constructedness), Ang contends that *Dallas* is best understood as an example of what she calls 'emotional realism'. Accordingly, *Dallas* can be read on two levels: the level of denotation (the literal content of the programme, general storyline, character interactions, etc.) and the level of connotation (the associations and implications which resonate from the storyline and character interactions, etc.).

> It is striking; the same things, people, relations and situations which are regarded at the denotative level as unrealistic, and unreal, are at the connotative level apparently not seen at all as unreal, but in fact as 'recognizable'. Clearly, in the connotative reading process the denotative level of the text is put in brackets. (42)

Viewing *Dallas*, like any other programme, is a selective process, reading across the text from denotation to connotation, weaving our sense of self in and out of the narrative. As one letter-writer says: '[d]o you know why I like watching it? I think it's because those problems and intrigues, the big and little pleasures and troubles occur in our own lives too . . . In real life I know a horror like J.R., but he's just an ordinary builder' (43). It is this ability to connect our own lives with the lives of a family of Texan millionaires which gives the programme its emotional realism. We may not be rich, but we have other fundamental things in common: relationships and broken relationships, happiness and sadness, illness and health. Those who find it realistic shift the focus of attention from the particularity of the (denotative) narrative to the generality of its (connotative) themes.

Given the way that *Dallas* plays with the emotions in an endless game of musical chairs in which happiness inevitably gives way to misery, Ang calls this a 'tragic structure of feeling' (46). As one letter-writer told her: '[s]ometimes I really enjoy having a good cry with them. And why not? In this way my other bottled-up emotions find an outlet' (49). Viewers who 'escape' in this way are not so much engaging in 'a denial of reality as playing with it . . . [in a] game that enables one to place the limits of the fictional and the real under discussion, to make them fluid. And in that game an imaginary participation in the fictional world is experienced as pleasurable' (49). Whatever else is involved, part of the pleasure(s) of *Dallas* is quite clearly connected to the amount of fluidity which viewers are able or willing to establish between its fictional world and the world of their day-to-day existence. But how does *Dallas* construct this tragic structure of feeling? Ang's answer is that it is 'the combination of melodramatic elements and the narrative structure of soap opera that evokes a tragic structure of feeling' (78). In order to activate this structure of feeling, it is necessary to have the cultural capital to take up a reading formation informed by what she calls (following Peter Brooks (1976)) the 'melodramatic imagination'. The melodramatic imagination is the articulation of a way of seeing beyond the grand human suffering of classical tragedy, to ordinary day-to-day existence, with its own pain and triumphs, its own victories and defeats, as itself profoundly meaningful and significant. It offers a means of organising reality, cut loose from the certainties of religion, into meaningful contrasts and conflicts. As a narrative form committed to melodrama's emphatic contrasts, conflicts and emotional excess, *Dallas* is well placed to give sustenance to and make manifest the melodramatic imagination. For those who see the world in this way (Ang claims that it demands a cultural competence most often shared by women), 'the pleasure of *Dallas* . . . is not a *compensation* for the presumed drabness of daily life, nor a *flight* from it, but a *dimension* of it' (83).

The melodramatic imagination activates what is perceived in the text as a tragic structure of feeling, which in turn produces the pleasure of emotional realism. As the melodramatic imagination is in effect a 'reading formation' (see chapter 3 below), it follows that not all viewers of *Dallas* will take up this particular reading position. On the basis of the letters, Ang is able to separate the viewers into three reading positions connected by what she calls 'the ideology of mass culture' (15). The ideology articulates (using the word in the Gramscian double sense to mean both to express and to form a relationship with) the view that popular culture is the product of capitalist commodity production and is therefore subject to the laws of the capitalist market economy; the result of which is the seemingly endless circulation of degraded commodities, whose only real significance is that they make a profit for their producers. The ideology of mass culture, like any ideological discourse, works by interpellating individuals into specific subject positions. The letters suggest three positions from which to consume *Dallas*: as fans, as ironical viewers, and as those who strongly dislike the programme.

Those letter-writers who strongly dislike *Dallas* draw most clearly on the ideology. They use it in two ways: to locate the programme negatively as an example of 'mass culture', and as a means to account for and support their dislike of the programme. As Ang puts it, 'their reasoning boils down to this: "*Dallas* is obviously bad because it's mass culture, and that's why I dislike it" ' (95–6). In this way, the ideology both comforts and reassures: 'it makes a search for more detailed and personal explanations superfluous, because it provides a finished explanatory model that convinces, sounds logical and radiates legitimacy' (96). This is not to say that it is wrong to dislike *Dallas*, only that professions of dislike are often made without thinking – in fact, with a confidence born of uncritical thought.

It is possible to like *Dallas* and still subscribe to the ideology of mass culture. The contradiction is resolved by 'mockery and irony' (97). *Dallas* is subjected to an ironising and mocking commentary in which it 'is transformed from a seriously intended melodrama to the reverse: a comedy to be laughed at. Ironising viewers therefore do not take the text as it presents itself, but invert its preferred meaning through ironic commentary' (98). In this construction, the pleasure of *Dallas* derives from the fact that it is bad: pleasure and bad mass culture are reconciled in an instant. As one of the letter-writers puts it: 'Of course *Dallas* is mass culture and therefore bad, but precisely because I am so well aware of that I can really enjoy watching it and poke fun at it' (100). For both the ironising viewer and the hater of *Dallas*, the ideology of mass culture operates as a bedrock of common sense, making judgements obvious and self-evident. Although both are trapped in the normative standards of the ideology, the difference between them is marked by the question of pleasure. On the one hand, the ironisers can have pleasure without guilt in the sure and declared knowledge that they know that mass culture is bad. On the other hand, the haters, although secure in the same knowledge, can, nevertheless, suffer 'a conflict of feelings if, *in spite of this*, they cannot escape its seduction' (101).

21

Finally, there are the fans, those who love *Dallas*. For the viewers who occupy the previous two positions, to actually like *Dallas* without resort to irony is to be identified as someone duped by mass culture. As one letter-writer puts it: 'The aim is simply to rake in money, lots of money. And people try to do that by means of all these things – sex, beautiful people, wealth. And you always have people who fall for it' (103). The claim is presented with all the confidence of having the full weight of the ideology's discursive support. Ang analyses the different strategies which the fans of *Dallas* must use to deal consciously and unconsciously with such condescension. The first strategy is to 'internalise' the ideology; to acknowledge the 'dangers' of *Dallas*, but to declare one's ability to deal with them in order to derive pleasure from the programme. Another strategy is to confront the ideology of mass culture as this letter-writer does: 'Many people find it worthless or without substance. But I think it does have substance' (105). But, as Ang points out, the writer remains firmly within the discursive constraints of the ideology as she attempts to relocate *Dallas* in a different relationship to the binary oppositions with substance/without substance, good/bad. 'This letter-writer "negotiates' as it were within the discursive space created by the ideology of mass culture, she does not situate herself outside it and does not speak from an opposing ideological position' (106). Finally, there is a letter which reveals a third strategy of defence against the normative standards of the ideology of mass culture. Like the second category of viewer, the ironist, this involves the use of surface irony; only this time irony is used to justify what is in all other respects a form of non-ironic pleasure. In this strategy, irony is used to condemn the characters as 'horrible' people, while at the same time demonstrating an intimate knowledge of the programme and a great involvement in its narrative development and character interactions, etc. She is caught between the dismissive power of the ideology and the pleasure which she obviously derives from watching *Dallas*. Her letter seems to suggest that she adheres to the former when viewing with friends, and to the latter when viewing alone (and perhaps secretly when viewing with friends). As Ang explains, 'irony is here a defence mechanism with which this letter-writer tries to fulfil the social norms set by the ideology of mass culture, while secretly she "really" likes *Dallas*' (109).

As Ang shows, the fans of *Dallas* find it necessary to locate their pleasure in relation to the ideology of mass culture; they 'internalise' the ideology; they 'negotiate' with the ideology; they use 'surface irony' to defend their pleasure against the withering dismissal of the ideology. What all these strategies of defence reveal is 'that there is no clear-cut ideological alternative which can be employed against the ideology of mass culture – at least no alternative that offsets the latter in power of conviction and coherence' (109–10). The struggle therefore, as so far described, between those who like *Dallas* and those who dislike it, is an unequal struggle between those who argue from within the discursive strength and security of the ideology of mass culture, and those who resist from within (for them) its inhospitable confines. 'In short, these fans do not seem to be able to take up an effective ideological position – an identity – from which they can say in a positive way and independently of the ideology of mass culture: "I like *Dallas* because . . ."' (110). There is, however, one final viewing position as revealed in the letters; one that might help these fans: that is, one informed by the ideology of populism. At the core of this ideology is the belief that one person's taste is of equal value to another person's taste. As one letter-writer puts it: 'I find the people who react oddly rather ludicrous – they can't do anything about someone's taste. And anyway they might find things pleasant that you just can't stand seeing or listening to' (113). The ideology of populism insists that as taste is an autonomous category, continually open to individual inflection, it is absolutely meaningless to pass aesthetic judgements on other people's preferences. Given that this would seem to be an ideal ideology from which to defend one's pleasure in *Dallas*, why do so few of the letter-writers adopt it? Ang's answer is that it is to do with the ideology's extremely limited vocabulary. After one has repeated 'there's no accounting for taste' a few times, the argument begins to appear rather limited. Compared to this, the ideology of mass culture has an extensive and elaborate range of arguments and theories. Little wonder, then, that when invited to explain why they like or dislike *Dallas*, the letter-writers find it difficult to escape the normative ideological discourse of mass culture.

Cultural studies, especially feminist cultural studies, must, according to Ang, break with the ideology of mass culture. She sees pleasure as the key concept in a transformed feminist cultural politics. Feminist cultural studies must struggle against 'the paternalism of the ideology of mass culture ... [in which w]omen are ... seen as the passive victims of the deceptive messages of soap operas ... [their] pleasure ... totally disregarded' (118–19). Pleasure should not be condemned as an obstruction to the feminist goal of women's liberation. The question which Ang poses is: can pleasure through identification with the women of 'women's weepies' or the emotionally masochistic women to soap operas 'have a meaning for women which is relatively independent of their political attitudes?' (133). Her answer is yes: fantasy and fiction do

> not function in place of, but beside, other dimensions of life (social practice, moral or political consciousness). It ... is a source of pleasure because it puts 'reality' in parenthesis, because it constructs imaginary solutions for real contradictions which in their fictional simplicity and their simple fictionality step outside the tedious complexity of the existing social relations of dominance and subordination. (135)

Of course this does not mean that representations of women do not matter. They can still be condemned for being reactionary in an ongoing cultural politics. But to experience pleasure from them is a completely different issue: 'it need not imply that we are also bound to take up these positions and solutions in our relations to our loved ones and friends, our work, our political ideals and so on' (135).

Fiction and fantasy, then, function by making life in the present pleasurable, or at least livable, but this does not by any means exclude radical political activity or consciousness. It does not follow that feminists must not persevere in trying to produce new fantasies and fight for a place for them . . . It does, however mean that, where cultural consumption is concerned, no fixed standard exists for gauging the 'progressiveness' of a fantasy. The personal may be political, but the personal and the political do not always go hand in hand. (135–6)

THE TWO ECONOMIES OF TELEVISION

John Fiske (1987) argues that cultural commodities – including television – from which popular culture is made circulate in two simultaneous economies: the financial and the cultural. The financial economy is primarily concerned with exchange value, the cultural is primarily focused on use – 'meanings, pleasures, and social identities' (311). There is of course continual interaction between these separate but related economies. Fiske gives the example of *Hill Street Blues*. The programme was made by MTM and sold to NBC, which then made a sponsorship deal with Mercedes Benz – in effect making the audience for *Hill Street Blues* available to Mercedes Benz. This all happened in the financial economy. In the cultural economy, the series changed from a cultural commodity (to be sold to NBC) to a site for the production of meanings and pleasures for its audience. In the same way, the audience changed from commodity (to be sold to Mercedes Benz) to a producer of meanings and pleasures.

Fiske insists 'that the power of audiences-as-producers in the cultural economy is considerable' (313). The power of the audience 'derives from the fact that meanings do not circulate in the cultural economy in the same way that wealth does in the financial' (313). While it is possible to possess wealth, it is much harder to possess meanings and pleasures. In the cultural economy – unlike in the financial economy – commodities do not move in a linear fashion from production to consumption; pleasures and meanings circulate without any real distinction between production and consumption. Moreover, the power of the consumer becomes manifest in the failure of producers to predict what will sell. 'Twelve out of thirteen records fail to make a profit, TV series are axed by the dozen, expensive films sink rapidly into red figures (*Raise the Titanic* is an ironic example – it nearly sank the Lew Grade empire)' (313).

In an attempt to offset the failures, the culture industries produce 'repertoires' of goods in the hope of attracting an audience. But audiences constantly engage in what Fiske calls – borrowing from Michel de Certeau (1984) – 'semiotic guerilla warfare' (316). Whereas the culture industries seek to incorporate audiences as commodity consumers, the audience often excorporates a television text, for example, for its own purposes. Fiske cites the example of the way in which Australian Aboriginal viewers appropriated Rambo as a figure of resistance, relevant to their own political and cultural struggles. He also cites the example of Russian Jews watching *Dallas* in Israel and reading it as 'capitalism's self-criticism' (320).

Fiske argues that resistance to the power of the powerful by those without power in Western societies takes two forms, semiotic and social. The first is mainly concerned with meanings, pleasures and social identities; the second, with transformations of the socio-economic system. He contends that 'the two are closely related, although relatively autonomous' (316). Popular culture operates mostly, 'but not exclusively', in the domain of semiotic power. It is involved in 'the struggle between homogenisation and difference, or between consensus and conflict' (316). In this sense, popular culture is a semiotic battlefield in which a conflict is fought out between the forces of incorporation and the forces of resistance, between an imposed set of meanings, pleasures and social identities, and the meanings, pleasures and social identities produced in acts of semiotic resistance: 'the hegemonic forces of homogeneity are always met by the resistances of heterogeneity' (Fiske 1989a: 8).

Fiske's two economies operate in the interests of opposing

sides of the struggle: the financial economy tends to favour the forces of incorporation and homogenisation, while the cultural economy tends to favour the forces of resistance and difference. Semiotic resistance – in which dominant meanings are challenged by subordinate meanings – has the effect of undermining capitalism's attempt at ideological homogeneity. In this way, according to Fiske, the dominant class's intellectual and moral leadership is challenged.

Fiske's approach to popular culture – including television – is one which recognises popular culture as 'a site of struggle' and, while acknowledging 'the power of the forces of dominance', chooses instead to direct its attention to 'the popular tactics by which these forces are coped with, are evaded or are resisted'. In other words, '[i]nstead of tracing exclusively the processes of incorporation, it investigates rather that popular vitality and creativity that makes incorporation such a constant necessity' (20). Moreover, 'instead of concentrating on the omnipresent, insidious practices of the dominant ideology, it attempts to understand the everyday resistances and evasions that make that ideology work so hard and insistently to maintain itself and its values'. His approach 'is essentially optimistic, for it finds in the vigour and vitality of the people evidence both of the possibility of social change and of the motivation to drive it (20–1).

NOTES

1. David Morley's *Family Television* (1986) discusses how television is in ways which render the term 'watching television' rather inadequate.
2. The essay was first presented as a paper to The Council of Europe Colloquy on 'Training in Critical Reading of Television Language', September 1973, and subsequently published as Centre for Contemporary Cultural Studies Stencilled Occasional Paper no. 7 in the same year. The diagram (Figure 1) and quotations are from Hall's 1980 revised version (Hall *et al.* 1980).
3. One interesting problem about the model is the way in which it seems always to assume encoding from a dominant position. What happens to the model when the encoded message is 'radical' or 'progressive'? See Dyer (1977).
4. Since the publication of *The 'Nationwide' Audience*, Morley has sought to both clarify and modify its theoretical and methodological claims.

For details see Morley 1980, 1986, 1992. For critical commentaries on the encoding/decoding model, and on Morley's use of it, see Ang 1989, Grossberg 1983, Jancovich 1992, Lewis 1983, Moores 1993, Turner 1990. See Cruz and Lewis 1994 for an interview with Stuart Hall on the encoding/decoding model.

3

FICTION

In *Culture and Environment* (first published in 1933), F. R. Leavis and Denys Thompson (1977) condemn popular fiction for offering addictive forms of 'compensation' and 'distraction'. Moreover, they add, '[t]his form of compensation . . . is the very reverse of recreation, in that it tends, not to strengthen and refresh the addict for living, but to increase his [sic] unfitness by habituating him to weak evasions, to the refusal to face reality at all' (100). Q. D. Leavis (1978), in *Fiction and the Reading Public* (first published in 1932), refers to such reading as 'a drug addiction to fiction' (152), adding that for those readers of romantic fiction it can lead to 'a habit of fantasying [which] will lead to maladjustment in actual life' (54). Self-abuse is bad enough, but there is worse: their addiction 'helps to make a social atmosphere unfavourable to the aspirations of the ["cultural"] minority. They actually get in the way of genuine feeling and responsible thinking' (74).

Half a century later, we witness a marked change in attitude. Here is Derek Longhurst (1989), introducing a collection of essays on popular fiction:

> It is now widely recognized that the study of popular fiction plays an important part in cultural analysis. No longer is reading popular fiction generally considered to be an activity

akin to a secret vice to which one should admit shamefacedly. Nor can popular narrative be adequately understood as merely narcotic and its readers as unenlightened junkies. (xi)

Although the distance between the elitist fantasies of the Leavisites and the cultural studies of Longhurst is immense and contains a story worth telling of theoretical and methodological battles won and lost, the rest of this chapter will focus instead on three significant approaches to the study of popular fiction in cultural studies: symptomatic reading, reading formations and romance reading.

IDEOLOGY AND SYMPTOMATIC READING

According to Louis Althusser (1969), ideological discourse is a closed system. As such, it can only ever set itself such problems as it can answer. To remain secure within its self-imposed boundaries, it must stay silent on questions which threaten to take it beyond these boundaries. This formulation leads Althusser to the concept of the 'problematic'. A problematic is the theoretical (and ideological) structure which both frames and produces the repertoire of criss-crossing and competing discourses out of which a text is materially organised. The problematic of a text relates to its moment of historical existence as much by what it excludes as by what it includes. That is to say, it encourages a text to answer questions posed by itself, but at the same time it generates the production of 'deformed' answers to the question which it attempts to exclude. Thus a problematic is structured as much by what is absent (what is not said) as by what is present (what is said). The task of critical practice is to deconstruct the text (read it symptomatically) to reveal the workings of its problematic and thus establish its relationship to its historical conditions of existence.

Althusser characterises Karl Marx's method of reading of the work of Adam Smith as 'symptomatic' in that

> it divulges the undivulged event in the text it reads, and in the same movement relates it to a *different text*, present as a necessary absence in the first. Like his first reading, Marx's second reading presupposes the existence of *two texts*, and

the measurement of the first against the second. But what distinguishes this new reading from the old is the fact that in the new one the second text is articulated with the lapses in the first text. (1979: 28)

By a symptomatic reading of Smith, Marx is able to measure 'the problematic initially visible in his writings against the invisible problematic contained in the paradox of *an answer which does not correspond to any question posed*' (28). Therefore, to read a text symptomatically is to perform a double reading: reading first the manifest text, and then, through the lapses and distortions, silences and absences (the 'symptoms' of a problem struggling to be posed) in the manifest text, to produce and read the latent text, the problematic.

Undoubtedly the most sustained attempt to apply this method of reading to fictional texts is Pierre Macherey's *A Theory of Literary Production* (1978). Macherey rejects what he calls 'the interpretative fallacy', the view that a text has a single meaning which it is the task of criticism to uncover. For him, the text is not a puzzle which conceals a meaning; it is a construction with a multiplicity of meanings. To 'explain' a text is to recognise this. Moreover, to do so it is necessary to break with the idea that a text is a harmonious unity spiralling forth from an 'original' moment of creation, a moment of supreme intentionality. Against this, he claims that the fictional text is 'decentred'; it is incomplete in itself. To say this does not mean that something needs to be added in order to make it whole. His point is that all fictional texts are 'decentred' (not centred on an authorial intention) in the specific sense in that they consist of a confrontation between several discourses: explicit, implicit, silent and absent. The task of critical practice is to explain the disparities in the text which point to a conflict of meanings.

> This conflict is not the sign of an imperfection; it reveals the inscription of an otherness in the work, through which it maintains a relationship with that which it is not, that which happens at its margins. To explain the work is to show that, contrary to appearances, it is not independent, but bears in its material substance the imprint of a determinate absence which

is also the principle of its identity. The book is furrowed by the allusive presence of those other books against which it is elaborated; it circles about the absence of that which it cannot say, haunted by the absence of certain repressed words which make their return. The book is not the extension of a meaning; it is generated from the incompatibility of several meanings, the strongest bond by which it is attached to reality, in a tense and ever-renewed confrontation. (79–80)

Macherey's approach should not be confused with one of literary criticism's traditional tasks – making explicit what is implicit in the text; making audible that which is merely a whisper (i.e. a single meaning). For Macherey, it is not a question of making what is there speak with more clarity so as to be finally sure of the text's meaning. Because a text's meanings are 'both interior and absent', to simply repeat the text's self-knowledge is to fail to really explain the text (78). The task of a fully competent critical practice is not to make a whisper audible, nor to complete what the text leaves unsaid, but to produce a new knowledge of the text, one that explains the ideological necessity of its silences, its absences, its structuring incompleteness – the *staging* of that which it cannot speak.

The act of knowing is not like listening to a discourse already constituted, a mere fiction which we have simply to translate. It is rather the elaboration of a new discourse, the articulation of a silence. Knowledge is not the discovery or reconstruction of a latent meaning, forgotten or concealed. It is something newly raised up, an addition to the reality from which it begins. (6)

Borrowing from Sigmund Freud's work on dreams, Macherey contends that in order for something to be said, other things must be left unsaid. It is the reason(s) for these absences, these silences, within a text which must be interrogated. 'What is important in the work is what it does not say' (87). Again, like Freud, who believed that the meanings of his patients' problems were not hidden in their conscious discourse but repressed in the turbulent discourse of the unconscious, necessitating a subtle form of analysis acute to the difference between what is said and what is shown, Macherey's approach explores the contradictions between telling and showing. He claims that there is always a 'gap', an 'internal distanciation', between what a text wants to say and what a text actually says. To explain a text, it is necessary to go beyond it, to understand what it 'is compelled to say in order to say what it wants to say' (94). It is here that the text's 'unconscious' (the Althusserian 'problematic') is constituted. And it is in a text's 'unconscious' that its relationship to the ideological and historical conditions of its existence is revealed. It is here, in the absent centre, hollowed out by conflicting discourses, that the text is related to history.

In a formal sense, a text always begins by posing a problem that is to be solved. The text then exists as a process of unfolding: the narrative movement to the final resolution of the problem. Macherey contends that between the problem posed and the resolution offered, rather than continuity, there is always a rupture. It is by examining this rupture that we discover the text's relationship with ideology and history: '[w]e always eventually find, at the edge of the text, the language of ideology, momentarily hidden, but eloquent by its very absence' (60). All narratives contain an ideological project. That is, they promise to tell the 'truth' about something. Information is initially withheld on the promise that it will be revealed. Narrative constitutes a movement towards disclosure. It begins with a truth promised and ends with a truth revealed. To be rather schematic, Macherey divides the text into three instances: the ideological project (the 'truth' promised), the realisation (the 'truth' revealed), and the 'unconscious' of the text (produced by an act of symptomatic reading): the return of the repressed; historical 'truth'.

The text's 'unconscious' does not reflect historical contradictions; rather, it evokes, stages and displays them, allowing us not a 'scientific' knowledge of ideology but an awareness of 'ideology in contradiction with itself' (130); breaking down before questions it cannot answer; failing to do what ideology is supposed to do – 'ideology exists precisely in order to efface all trace of contradiction' (131). 'Science', according to Macherey, destroys ideology; the fictional text challenges ideology by using it, making it visible and therefore available to analysis and contestation. In his discussion, for example, of the work of the French popular science-fiction writer Jules Verne, he shows how Verne's work *stages* the contradictions of late nineteenth-century French imperialism. He contends that the ideological project of Verne's work is the *fantastic* staging of the adventures of French imperialism: its colonising conquest of the earth. Each adventure concerns the hero's conquest of Nature (a mysterious island, the moon, the bottom of the sea, the centre of the earth). In telling these stories, Verne is 'compelled' to tell another: each voyage of conquest becomes a voyage of rediscovery as Verne's heroes discover that others have either been there before or are there already. The significance of this, for Macherey, lies in the disparity which he perceives between 'representation' (what is intended: the subject of the narrative) and 'figuration' (how it is realised: its inscription in narrative): Verne 'represents' the ideology of French imperialism, while at the same time, through the act of 'figuration' (making material in the *form* of a fiction), undermines one of its central myths in the continual staging of the fact that the lands are always already occupied. 'In the passage from the level of representation to that of figuration, ideology undergoes a complete *modification* . . . perhaps because no ideology is sufficiently consistent to survive the test of figuration' (194–5). Thus, by giving fictional form to the ideology of imperialism, Verne's work ('to read it against the grain of its intended meaning') (230) stages the contradictions between the myth and the reality of imperialism. The stories do not provide us with a 'scientific' denunciation ('a knowledge in the strict sense') of imperialism, but by an act of symptomatic reading 'which dislodges the work internally' (161) they 'make us see', 'make us perceive', 'make us feel' the terrible contradictions of the ideological discourses from which each text of Verne's is constituted: 'from which it is born, in which it bathes, from which it detaches itself . . . and to which it alludes' (Althusser 1971: 222). Verne's science-fantasy adventure stories show us – though not in the way(s) intended – the ideological and historical conditions of their existence.

READING FORMATIONS

The general focus of Tony Bennett's and Janet Woollacott's (1987) *Bond and Beyond* is the diverse and changing ways in which the figure of James Bond has been produced and reproduced through a range of different cultural texts and practices. Analysis ranges from the novels and films to academic criticism, showbiz journalism, fanzine articles, advertising copy and interviews with stars and film-makers, to chart the different and changing ways in which 'the figure of Bond has been put into circulation as a popular hero' (1).

Bennett and Woollacott reject the view that the texts of popular fiction are little more than containers of ideology, a convenient and always successful means to transmit dominant ideology from the culture industries to the duped and manipulated masses. The problem with such a view is that it leads to 'a politics of simple opposition and to a criticism which is little more than a constant unmasking of dominant ideologies at work' (4). Against this, they contend that popular fiction is a specific space, with its own ideological economy, making available a historically variable, complex and contradictory range of ideological discourses and counter-discourses to be activated in particular conditions of reading. While they accept that it may be possible to describe the Bond novels and films as racist, sexist and reactionary, to stop there is to fail to explore how these texts engage with a popular audience. That is, of course, 'Unless one subscribes to the view that the reading, cinema-going and television publics simply enjoy sexist, racist and reactionary texts' (4). Rather than simply condemn these texts, Bennett and Woollacott seek to explore why and how they make their appeal.

James Bond is undoubtedly fiction's most famous spy. The popularity of Bond (certainly during the 1950s, and 1960s and 1970s) is beyond question. By 1977, the worldwide audience for Bond films was in excess of 1,000 million, while paperback sales in Britain alone totalled 27,863,500. It is Bennett and Woollacott's contention that

Bond's popularity resulted from his ability to articulate – to connect and to express – a series of cultural and political concerns. These include the historically mobile ideological relations between West and East, capitalism and communism, masculine and feminine, as well as changing notions of Englishness.

> However, the precise way in which the figure of Bond has articulated – that is, connected and expressed – these concerns has varied during different moments of his career as a popular hero. The ideological and cultural elements out of which the figure of Bond has been woven may have been constant, but these have been combined in different mixes and shifting permutations. If Bond has functioned as a 'sign of the times', it has been as a *moving sign of the times*, as a figure capable of taking up and articulating quite different and even contradictory cultural and ideological values, sometimes turning its back on the meanings and cultural possibilities it had earlier embodied to enunciate new ones. (19)

Moreover, it is the ideological 'malleability' of the figure of Bond which has ensured his continuing popularity. As Bennett and Woollacott point out, 'it is not the popularity of *Bond* that has to be accounted for so much as the popularity of *different Bonds*, popular in different ways and for different reasons at different points in time' (20). What has remained constant is the way in which Bond 'has functioned as a shifting focal point for the articulation of historically specific ideological concerns' (20).

Bond's first moment of popularity occurs in the late 1950s. The key events are the paperback publication of *Casino Royale* and *Moonraker*, and the serialisation of *From Russia, With Love* in the *Daily Express*, followed by a daily strip-cartoon of Bond in the same newspaper. Sales of the novels in Britain rose from 58,000 in 1956 to 237,000 in 1959. During this period, Bond served as a political hero of the lower middle class.

> Bond . . . functioned first and foremost, although not exclu-sively, as a Cold War hero, an exemplary representative of the virtues of Western capitalism triumphing over the evils of

Eastern communism . . . Bond effects an ideologically loaded imaginary resolution of the real historical contradictions of the period, a resolution in which all the values associated with Bond and, thereby, the West – notably, freedom and individualism – gain ascendancy over those associated with the villain and, thereby, communist Russia, such as totalitarianism and bureaucratic rigidity. (25)

In addition, given that this is the period following the blow to national dignity represented by the fiasco of Suez (1956), it is not surprising that the figure of Bond also articulates an appeal to a more mythic notion of English nationhood. As above all an *English* hero, in a period of marked national decline, Bond seemed to offer the promise of a turning-back of history and a return to a time of world leadership. What could no longer be achieved in the real world might be symbolically brought into play in the fictional world of James Bond.

The second moment of Bond occurs in the early 1960s, with the release of the first Bond film, *Dr No*. The effect was twofold. First, it broadened the social base of Bond's popularity. Second, it entailed the 'ideological remodelling' (30) of the figure of Bond. As Bennett and Woollacott explain,

The various ideological and cultural elements out of which the figure of Bond had earlier been constructed were, so to speak, dismantled and separated from one another in order to be reassembled in a new configuration which pointed, ideologically and culturally, in a number of new and different directions. (30)

The release of the first cycle of Bond films (*Dr No*, 1962; *From Russia, With Love*, 1963; *Goldfinger*, 1964; *Thunderball*, 1965; *You Only Live Twice*, 1967) increased the sales of the novels. It also brought the figure of Bond into the world of advertising and commodity production. But more than this, it modified Bond's ideological and cultural significance. First, it relocated Bond in terms of East–West relations, moving him from Cold War hero to defender of détente. In narrative terms, this meant the replacement of SMERSH by SPECTRE. The enemy was no longer the communist East but an international criminal conspiracy, determined to exploit the still fragile relations between capitalist West and communist East. Second, Bond's Englishness no longer represented an attempt to put history in reverse, but increasingly became a symbol of the nation running in advance of history – the embodiment of the values of 'swinging Britain'.

> Bond provided a mythic encapsulation of the then promi-
> nent ideological themes of classlessness and modernity, a
> key cultural marker of the claim that Britain had escaped
> the blinkered, class-bound perspectives of its traditional
> ruling elites and was in the process of being thoroughly
> modernised as a result of the implementation of a new,
> meritocratic style of cultural and political leadership, middle-
> class and professional rather than aristocratic and amateur.
> (34–5)

Whereas, in the first moment, Bond's individualism was set in opposition to the mundane bureaucracy of the communist countries of the East, his individualism now signalled the meritocratic culture of a 'classless' Britain, 'swinging' free of the dead weight of the past and 'the allegedly morally sapping effects of welfare socialism' (237). Thus the figure of Bond moved from being a hero of tradition to become a hero of progress, from the past to the promise of the future, as the first cycle of films adjusted the inter-textual relations in which Bond figured as a popular hero.

The third modification to Bond's ideological currency during this period is the bringing into play, together with the new figure of 'the Bond girl', of a new construction of gender and sexual relations.

> Between them, Bond and 'the Bond girl' embodied a modern
> isation of sexuality, representatives of norms of masculinity
> and femininity that were 'swinging free' from the constraints
> of the past. If Bond thus embodied a male sexuality that

38

was freed from the constraints and hypocrisy of gentle-manly chivalry, a point of departure from the restraint, a-sexuality or repressed sexuality of the traditional English aristocratic hero, 'the Bond girl' – tailored to suit Bond's needs – was likewise represented as the subject of a free and independent sexuality, liberated from the constraints of family, marriage and domesticity. The image of 'the Bond girl' thus constituted a model of adjustment, a con-densation of the attributes of femininity appropriate to the requirements of the new norms of male sexuality represented by Bond.(35)

The third moment of Bond's career as a popular hero, from the 1970s onwards, is marked by a selective and strategic activation of Bond's already established ideological currency. Bond's popularity is now institutionalised as family entertainment. Still a figure in advertising and commodity production, he is no longer marketed in terms of sexuality or nationhood but through the technology increasingly highlighted in the Bond films – spin-off items aimed at children. There is also a significant contraction in terms of Bond's ideological range. The political concerns of East–West relations and the articulation of Englishness remain, but mostly to be mocked and parodied. The central ideological focus is now gender and sexuality.

The most significant change associated with the films of this period . . . consisted in a shift in the centre of narrative interest, increasingly pronounced as the 1970s progressed, away from the relations between Bond and the villain towards the relations between Bond and 'the Bond girl'. Usually portrayed as 'excessively' independent – a fellow professional who works alongside Bond, threatening to best him in the traditionally masculine preserve of espionage work, . . . the destiny of 'the Bond girl' in the films of this period is to meet her come-uppance in her encounter with Bond. The main ideological work thus accomplished in the unfolding of the narrative is that of a 'putting-back-in-place' of women who carry their independence and liberation 'too far' or into 'inappropriate' fields of activity. (39)

This is not a new concern (it's there in the novels and the early films). However, what is new is the dominant place which this concern now occupies in the narrative structure, subordinating all other concerns. This change in narrative focus 'clearly constituted a response – in truth, somewhat nervous and uncertain – to the Women's Liberation movement, fictitiously rolling back the advances of feminism to restore an imaginarily more secure phallocentric conception of gender relations' (39). 'It can thus be seen that the figure of Bond has been differently constructed at different moments in the Bond phenomenon. 'James Bond' has been a variable and mobile signifier rather than one that can be fixed as unitary and constant in its signifying functions and effects' (42).

The point of discussing the films is not simply to draw attention to how they produced a popular readership for the novels. What is of crucial theoretical and methodological interest are the ways in which the films (and other 'texts of Bond') helped to organise and predispose 'readers to read the novels in certain ways, privileging some of their aspects at the expense of others' (43). At the centre of Bennett's and Woollacott's argument is the claim that 'the condition of Bond's existence have been *inter-textual*' (44). They use the hyphen to indicate the theoretical difference between their usage of the term and the way in which the term is usually employed (without the hyphen) within cultural studies to signify the way in which one text is marked by the signs of other texts. As Bennett and Woollacott make clear, their employment of the term is quite different: 'we intend the concept inter-textuality to refer to the social organisation of the relations between texts within specific conditions of reading' (45). Moreover, they argue that 'the latter overrides and overdetermines the former. *Intertextualities* . . . are the product of specific, socially organised *inter-textualities*; it is the latter which, in providing the objective determinants of reading practices, provide the framework within which inter-textual references can be produced and operate' (86). Thus, they argue,

> The figure of Bond has been produced in the constantly changing relations between the wide range of texts brought into association with one another via the functioning of Bond as the signifier which they have jointly constructed. In turn, it is this figure which, in floating between them, has thereby connected these texts into a related set in spite of their manifold differences in other respects. (45)

In other words, what unites these texts is not an author (even the novels are written by a number of authors), but the figure of Bond. It is Bond who 'furnishes the operative principle of textual classification' (52). Moreover, when Bond changes, 'such changes form a part of the social and cultural determination which influence the way the texts concerned are available to be read' (52–3). An objection to this argument might be to claim that the novels (as the original source of Bond) have a privileged status over the other 'texts of Bond'. Bennett and Woollacott claim that such an argument 'is impossible to maintain' (53).

> The 'texts of Bond' have comprised a constantly accumulating and 'mutating' set of texts, 'mutating' in the sense that additions to the set have connected with the pre-existing 'texts of Bond' in such a way as to reorganise kaleidoscopically the relationships, transactions and exchanges between them. None of the texts in which the figure of Bond has been constructed can thus be regarded as privileged in relation to the others in any absolute or permanent sense. Rather, each region of this textual set occupies a privileged position in relation to the others, but in different ways depending on the part it has played in the circulation and expanded reproduction of the figure of Bond. (54)

Therefore, although Fleming's novels came first and supplied much of the material for the subsequent films, once the films were in circulation it was these that dominated constructions of the figure of Bond. As noted earlier, it was the films which produced the popular audience for the novels. But more than this, Bennett and Woollacott would insist, it was the films which provided the interpretative framework through which to read the novels. Once this is acknowledged, the rather one-way relationship (questions of difference and similarity, etc.) usually brought into play in discussions of film adaptations of novels begins to look unconvincing. As Bennett and Woollacott contend, the films 'have culturally activated the novels in particular ways, selectively cueing their reading, modifying the exchange between text and reader, inflecting it in new directions by inserting the novels within an expanded inter-textual set' (55).

The point can be illustrated by considering how different Bond might appear to a reader who reads the novels (pre-film adaptations) as belonging to the tradition of the imperialist spy-thriller as against the reader who reads them having seen the first cycle of Bond films.[1] Neither would produce the 'true' response; no more so than, say, the American readers who located the novels in the tradition of hard-boiled fiction or the romance readers who read Bond as a classic romantic hero. What these possible readings point to is the way in which reading is always

> profoundly affected by the reader's specific preorientation to the novels produced by his or her insertion in the orders of inter-textuality which, in different ways for different groups of readers in different circumstances, hover between text and reader, connecting the two within specific horizons of intelligibility. The process of reading is not one in which reader and text meet as abstractions but one in which the inter-textually organised reader meets the inter-textually organised text. The exchange is never a pure one between two unsullied entities, existing separately from one another, but is rather 'muddied' by the cultural debris which attach to both texts and readers in the determinate conditions which regulate the specific forms of their encounter . . . The Bond novels now reach us already humming with the meanings established by the films and, as a consequence, have been hooked into orders of inter-textuality to which, initially, they were not connected. (56)

Bennett and Woollacott reject both the view that the text determines its own reading (invites recognition of its objective properties) and the apparently contrary view that it is the reader who produces the meaning of the text. They accuse both approaches of working with a 'metaphysical view of texts' (60), in that the first claims that the meaning of a text pre-exists its conditions of reading, while the second, although accepting the possibility of variable readings, nonetheless insists that these are variable readings of the *same* text. Against both of these positions, they argue for a rethinking of the text–reader relationship.

> This entails that these texts [the Bond novels] be conceived as having no existence prior to or independently of the varying 'reading formations' in which they have been constituted as objects-to-be-read. By 'reading formations' here, we have in mind not the generalised cultural determinations of reading considered by David Morley [see chapter 2 above], but those specific determinations which bear in upon, mould and configure the relations between texts and readers in determinant conditions of reading. It refers, specifically, to the inter-textual relations which prevail in a particular context, thereby activating a given body of texts by ordering the relations between them in a specific way such that their reading is always-already cued in specific directions that are not given by those 'texts themselves' as entities separable from such relations. (64)

Bennett and Woollacott contend that both texts and readers are 'always-already culturally activated' (64) to the extent that the distinction between subject and object is continually blurred. As they contend, 'text and reader are conceived as being co-produced within a reading formation, gridded on to one another in a determinate compact unity' (64). In other words, a text only becomes a text when read, just as a reader only becomes a reader in the act of reading; neither can exist outside this relationship. This of course exposes Bennett and Woollacott to the accusation that they are claiming that readers and texts have no objective existence. They clarify as follows:

> This is not to suggest that texts have no determinate properties – such as a definite order of narrative progression – which

may be analysed objectively. But it is to argue that such properties cannot, in themselves, validate certain received meanings above others; they do not provide a point of 'truth' in relation to which readings may be normatively and hierarchically ranked, or discounted. Nor are we suggesting that readers do not have determinate properties. They most certainly do, but complexly varying ones which, rather than being attributable to the reader as a subject independent of the text, are the product of the orders of inter-textuality which have marked the reader's formation. (65)

Bennett and Woollacott's purpose in detailing the different moments in the construction of Bond as a popular hero is not to make claims about the 'true' meaning of Bond. 'On the contrary', as they explain, 'we have contended that neither the meanings nor the meaning-producing structures of texts can be specified independently of the reading formations which regulate reading practices' (141–2). Regimes of inter-textuality organise how readers read texts. We never get access to texts 'in themselves', but always as situated within a network of inter-textual relations.

We have thus, in approaching the various individual 'texts of Bond', stressed the degree to which these have always been variably produced – not as 'the same text' but as different 'texts-to-be-read' – as a result of their insertion within different regimes of inter-textuality. Further, we have suggested that it is not possible to abstract any of the individual texts of Bond from the mobile and changing systems of inter-textual relationships through which their reading has been organised in order to constitute a space in which such texts might be stabilised as possible objects of knowledge 'in themselves'. (260–1)

In other words, text and context are not separate moments available for analysis at different times. Text and context are always part of the same process, the same moment – they are inseparable: one cannot have a text without a context, or context without a text. Moreover, Bennett and Woollacott contend that all previous approaches to question of meaning-production have assumed that one can separate textual meaning from the meanings produced in actual acts of reading. The first supposedly approximates to the essential properties of the text (and can be determined without reference to factors outside or beyond the text); the second, influenced (muddled and blurred) by extra-textual variables, may change through history and across cultures, but it is still a reading of (a variation on) the essential properties of the text (in other words, different readings of the same text). This is a mode of analysis, which, despite its reference to the activities of readers, always ends up privileging the text. There is an objective structure and there is the endless flow of subjective responses. Drawing on the work of the French linguist. Michel Pécheux, Bennett and Woollacott argue that meaning (or reading) does not exist prior to its articulation by a reader. It cannot pre-exist the encounter between reader and text. This is not an attempt to reduce text to context, but an insistence that context and text cannot be conceived of as separate entities. 'The concept of reading formation . . . is an attempt to think of contexts of reception as sets of discursive and inter-textual determinations which, in operating on both texts and readers, mediate the relations between them and provide the mechanisms through which they can productively interact' (263). They do not deny that texts have a material existence. But they do insist that the most adequate way to conceive of a text is 'as a historically constituted object rather than as a metaphysical essence' (266).

Similarly, they also insist that we must distinguish between the subject positions offered by texts and the 'social subject' who may or may not take up the invitation offered. In addition, they contend that the subject positions offered by texts 'only exist in relation to regimes of inter-textuality, within which "social subjects" exist and from which they read texts' (229). Subjects are not constructed by texts, but by regimes of inter-textuality.

Much previous debate on the question of reading has dead-locked on the opposition between the view of the text as dictating its readings and the view that readers are able to mobilise cultural resources which enable them to read against the grain of the text or to negotiate its meanings in particular ways. Our purpose has been to displace the terms of this dispute by suggesting that neither approach takes sufficient account of the cultural and ideological forces which organise and reorganise the network of inter-textual relations within which texts are inserted as texts-to-be-read in certain ways by reading subjects organised to read in certain ways. The relations between texts and readers, we have suggested, are always profoundly mediated by the discursive and inter-textual determinations which, operating on both, structure the domain of their encounter so as to produce, always in specific and variable forms, texts and readers as the mutual supports of one another. (249)

READING ROMANTIC FICTION

In *Loving with a Vengeance*, Tania Modleski (1982) claims that women writing about 'feminine narratives' tend to adopt one of three possible positions: 'dismissiveness; hostility – tending unfortunately to be aimed at the consumers of the narratives; or, most frequently, a flippant kind of mockery' (14). Against this, she declares: '[i]t is time to begin a feminist reading of women's reading' (34). She argues that these popular narratives 'speak to very real problems and tensions in women's lives' (14). Despite this, she acknowledges that the way in which these narratives resolve problems and tensions will rarely 'please modern feminists: far from it' (25). However, the reader of fantasies and the feminist reader do have something in common: dissatisfaction with women's lives.

Rosalind Coward's (1984) interest in romantic fiction is in part inspired by the claim that '[o]ver the past decade, the rise of feminism has been paralleled almost exactly by a mushroom growth in the popularity of romantic fiction' (190). Coward believes two things about romantic fiction: that 'they must still satisfy some very definite needs', and that they offer evidence of, and contribute to, 'a very powerful and common fantasy' (190). She claims that the fantasies played out in romantic fiction are 'pre-adolescent, very nearly pre-conscious' (191–2). She believes them to be 'regressive' in two key respects. On the one hand, they adore the power of the male in ways reminiscent of the very early child-father relationship, while on the other, they are regressive because of the attitude taken to female sexual desire – passive and without guilt, as the responsibility for sexual desire is projected on the male; sexual desire is something that men have and to which women merely respond. In short, romantic fiction replays the girl's experience of the Oedipal drama, only this time without its conclusion in female powerlessness; this time she does marry the father and replace the mother. Therefore there is a trajectory from subordination to position of power (as the mother figure). But, as Coward points out,

> [r]omantic fiction is surely popular because it . . . restores the childhood world of sexual relations and suppresses criticisms of the inadequacy of men, the suffocation of the family, or the damage inflicted by patriarchal power. Yet it simultaneously manages to avoid the guilt and fear which might come from that childhood world. Sexuality is defined firmly as the father's responsibility, and fear of suffocation is overcome because women achieve a sort of power in romantic fiction. Romantic fiction promises a secure world, promises that there will be safety with dependence, that there will be power with subordination. (196)

Janice Radway's *Reading the Romance* (1987) has been described by Charlotte Brunsdon (1991) as 'the most extensive scholarly investigation of the act of reading', crediting Radway with having installed in the classroom '[t]he figure of the ordinary woman' (372). Radway's study is based on research she carried out in 'Smithton', involving a group of forty-two romance readers (mostly married with children). Her research was conducted through individual question-naires, open-ended group discussions, face-to-face interviews, some informal discussions, and by observing the interactions between the different members of Smithton's symbolic community of romance readers.

According to the Smithton women, the ideal romance is one in which an intelligent and independent woman with a good sense of humour is overwhelmed, after much suspicion and distrust, and some cruelty and violence, by the love of an intelligent, tender and good-humoured man, who in the course of their relationship is transformed from an emotional pre-literate to someone who can *care* for her and *nurture* her in ways that traditionally we would expect only from a woman to a man. As Radway explains: '[t]he romantic fantasy is . . . not a fantasy about discovering a uniquely interesting life partner, but a ritual which to be cared for, loved, and validated in a particular way' (83). It is a fantasy about reciprocation; the wish to believe that men can bestow on women the care and attention that women are expected regularly to bestow on men. But the romantic fantasy offers more than this; it recalls a time when the reader was in fact the recipient of an intense 'material' care. Drawing on the work of Nancy Chodorow (1978), Radway claims that romantic fantasy is a form of regression in which the reader is imaginatively and emotionally transported to a time 'when she was the center of a profoundly nurturant individual's attention' (84). Romance reading, Radway argues, is a fantasy in which the hero is eventually the source of care and attention not experienced by the reader since she was a pre-Oedipal child. In this way, romance reading can be viewed as a means by which women can vicariously, through the hero–heroine relationship, experience the emotional succour which they themselves are expected to provide to others without adequate reciprocation for themselves in their normal day-to-day existence.

Radway also takes from Chodorow the notion of the female self as a self-in-relation to others, and the male self as a self autonomous and independent. Chodorow argues that this results from the different relations that a girl and boy have with their mother. Radway sees a correlation between the psychological events described by Chodorow and the narrative pattern of the ideal romance: in the journey from identity in crisis to identity restored, 'the heroine successfully establishes by the end of the ideal narrative . . . the now-familiar female self, the self-in-relation' (134). Radway also takes from Chodorow the belief that women emerge from the Oedipal complex with a 'triangular psychic structure intact'. The result is that 'not only do they need to connect themselves with a member of the opposite sex, but they also continue to require an intense emotional bond with someone who is reciprocally nurturant and protective in a maternal way' (140). In order to experience this regression to maternal emotional fulfilment, she has three options: lesbianism, a relationship with a man, or to seek fulfilment by other means. The homophobic nature of our culture limits the first; the nature of masculinity limits the second; romance reading may be an example of the third. Radway contends that

> the fantasy that generates the romance originates in the oedipal desire to love and be loved by an individual of the opposite sex *and* in the continuing pre-oedipal wish that is part of a woman's inner-object configuration, the wish to regain the love of the mother and all that it implies – erotic pleasure, symbotic completion, and identity confirmation. (146)

The resolution to the ideal romance provides perfect triangular satisfaction: 'fatherly protection, motherly care, and passionate adult love' (149)

The failed romance is unable to provide these satisfactions because on the one hand it is too violent, and on the other it concludes sadly, or with an unconvincing happy ending. This highlights in an unpleasurable way the two structuring anxieties of all romances. The first is the fear of male violence. In the ideal romance, this is contained by revealing it to be not the fearful thing it appears to be; it is either an illusion or benign. The second anxiety is the 'fear of an awakened female sexuality and its impact on men' (169). In the failed romance, female sexuality is not confined to a permanent and loving relationship; nor is male violence convincingly brought under control. Together they find form and expression in the violent punishment inflicted on women who are seen as sexually promiscuous. In short, the failed romance is unable to produce a reading experience in which emotional fulfilment is satisfied through the vicarious sharing of the heroine's journey from a crisis of identity to an identity restored in the arms of a nurturing male. Whether a romance is good or bad is ultimately determined by the kind of relationship the reader can establish with the heroine.

> If the events of the heroine's story provoke too intense feelings such as anger at men, fear of rape and violence, worry about female sexuality, or worry about the need to live with an unexciting man, that romance will be discarded as a failure or judged to be very poor. If, on the other hand, those events call forth feelings of excitement, satisfaction, contentment, self-confidence, pride, and power, it matters less what events are used or how they are marshalled. In the end, what counts most is the reader's sense that for a short time she has become other and been elsewhere. She must close that book reassured that men and marriage really do mean good things for women. She must also turn back to her daily round of duties, emotionally reconstituted and replenished, feeling confident of her worth and convinced of her ability and power to deal with the problem she knows she must confront. (184)

Radway claims that by engaging in this process of discrimination, the Smithton women are taking emotional benefits for themselves where other critics see only financial benefits for the publishing industry. The Smithton women 'partially reclaim the patriarchal form of the romance for their own use' (184). The principal 'psychological benefits' derive from 'the ritualistic repetition of a single, immutable cultural myth' (199, 198). The fact that 60 per cent of the Smithton readers find it occasionally necessary to read the ending first to ensure that the experience of the novel won't counteract the satisfactions of the underlying myth suggests quite strongly that it is the underlying myth of the nurturing male that is ultimately of most importance in the Smithton women's experience of romance reading.

Following a series of comments from the Smithton women, Radway was forced to the conclusion that if she really wished to understand their view of romance reading, she had to relinquish her preoccupation with the text and consider also the very *act of romance reading* itself. In conversations, it became clear that when the women used the term 'escape' to describe the pleasure of romance reading, the term was operating in a double but related sense. As we have seen, it can be used to describe the process of identification between the reader and the heroine–hero relationship. But it became clear that the term was also used 'literally to describe the act of denying the present, which they believe they accomplish each time they begin to read a book and are drawn into its story' (90). Many of the Smithton women describe romance reading as 'a special gift' that they give themselves. It is seen as time reclaimed from the demands of family and domestic duties that they otherwise perform willingly. For this reason, some Smithton men find the very act of women reading a threat to their patriarchal authority. Romance reading is for the Smithton women 'a temporary but literal denial of the demands women recognize as an integral part of their roles as nurturing wives and mothers' (97). And, as Radway suggests, '[a]lthough this experience *is* vicarious, the pleasure it induces is nonetheless real' (100).

> I think it is logical to conclude that romance reading is valued by the Smithton women because the experience itself is *different* from ordinary existence. Not only is it a relaxing release from the tension produced by daily problems and responsibilities, but it creates a time or a space within which a woman can be entirely on her own, preoccupied with her personal needs, desires, and pleasure. It is also a means of transportation or escape to the exotic, or, again, to that which is different. (61)

Romance reading pulls in different 'political' directions, depending on whether the focus is the act of reading or the narrative fantasies of the texts themselves. The first suggests that 'romance reading is oppositional because it allowed the women to refuse momentarily their self-abnegating social role' (210). The second suggests 'that the romance's narrative structure embodies a simple recapitulation and recommendation of patriarchy and its constituent social practices and ideologies' (210). It is this difference, 'between the meaning of the act and the meaning of the text as read', that must be brought into tight focus if we are to understand the full meaning of romance reading (210).

On one thing Radway is clear: women do not read romances out of a sense of contentment with patriarchy. Romance reading contains an element of utopian protest, a longing for a better world. But against this, the narrative structure of the romance appears to suggest that male violence and male indifference are really expressions of love waiting to be decoded by the right woman. This suggests that patriarchy is only a problem until women learn how to read it properly. It is these complexities and contradictions which Radway refuses to ignore or pretend to resolve. Her only certainty is that it is too soon to know if romance reading can be cited simply as an ideological agent of the patriarchal status quo.

> I feel compelled to point out . . . that neither this study nor any other to date provides enough evidence to corroborate this argument fully. We simply do not know what practical effects the repetitive reading of romances has on the way women behave after they have closed their books and returned to their normal, ordinary round of daily activities. (217)

Therefore we must continue to acknowledge the activity of readers – their selections, purchases, interpretations, appropriations, uses, etc. – as an essential part of the cultural process and complex practice of making meaning. By paying attention in this way, we increase the possibility of 'articulating the differences between the repressive imposition of ideology and oppositional practices that, though limited in their scope and effect, at least dispute or contest the control of ideological forms' (221–2). The ideological power of romances may be great, but where there is power there is always resistance. The resistance may be confined to selective acts of consumption; dissatisfactions momentarily satisfied by the articulation of limited protest and utopian longing. But, as feminists,

> [w]e should seek it out not only to understand its origins and its utopian longing but also to learn how best to encourage it and bring it to fruition. If we do not, we have already conceded

the fight and, in the case of the romance at least, admitted the impossibility of creating a world where the vicarious pleasure supplied by its reading would be unnecessary. (222)

NOTE

1. Bennett and Woollacott give the example of Ian Fleming commenting on Sean Connery as Bond (Fleming's preferred choice was David Niven): 'Not quite the idea I had of Bond, but he would be if I wrote the books again' (57).

4

FILM

Film studies has generated a wide range of theories and methods. It has been studied in terms of its potential as 'art', its history told as moments in a 'great tradition', the most significant films, stars and directors; it has been analysed in terms of the changing technology of film production; it has been condemned as a culture industry; and it has been discussed as a key site for the production of individual subjectivities and national identities. This is not, however, a chapter on recent developments in film studies, nor is it even an account of the study of popular film. Rather, the aim is more limited: to discuss a series of key moments in the relationship between the study of popular film and the development of cultural studies.

STRUCTURALISM AND POPULAR FILM

In the 1970s, there developed a clear divide within cultural studies between the study of 'texts' and the study of 'lived cultures'. If the object of study was texts, the method of analysis was structuralism. As a result, film studies within cultural studies was dominated by structuralism. In 1975, two important contributions to structuralism and film were published: Will Wright's *Sixguns and Society* and Laura Mulvey's 'Visual Pleasure and Narrative

Cinema'. The first is anchored in classical structuralism; the second represents the first significant exploration of poststructuralism and cinema.

Structuralism is a theoretical method derived from the theoretical work of the Swiss linguist Ferdinand de Saussure (1974). Saussure divides language into two component parts, which together produce a third. When I write the word 'cat', it produces the inscription 'cat', but also the concept or mental image of a cat: a four-legged feline creature. Saussure calls the first the 'signifier', and the second the 'signified'. Together (like two sides of a sheet of paper) they make up the 'sign'. Saussure argues that the relationship between signifier and signified is arbitrary. The word 'cat' has no cat-like qualities, there is no necessary reason why the signifier 'cat' should produce the signified 'cat': four-legged feline creature. The relationship between the two is simply the result of convention – of cultural agreement. The signifier 'cat' could just as easily produce the signified 'dog': four-legged canine creature. Saussure also contends that meaning is not the result of an essential correspondence between signifiers and signifieds, it is rather the result of difference and relationship. The signifier 'cat' means the signified 'cat' because the signifier is not 'mat', 'rat' or 'sat', for example. Language is for Saussure a system of contrasts and opposites.

According to Saussure, then, meaning is produced through a process of combination and selection. Rather than reflecting an already existing reality, the function of language is to organise and construct our access to reality. Therefore different languages will organise and construct the world differently. Eskimos are said to have over fifty words to describe snow. Therefore an Eskimo and a European standing together surveying the same snowscape would in fact be seeing two quite different conceptual scenes. What this demonstrates to a structuralist is that the way in which we conceptualise the world is ultimately dependent on the language that we speak and, by analogy, the culture that we inhabit. The meanings made possible by language are thus the result of the interplay of a network of relationships between combination and selection, similarity and difference. Meaning cannot be accounted for by reference to an extra-linguistic reality. As Saussure insists, 'in langauge there are only differences *without positive terms* . . . language has neither ideas not sounds that existed before the linguistic system, but only conceptual and phonic differences that have issued for the system' (1974: 120).

Saussure makes another distinction which has proved essential to the development of structuralism, the division of language into 'langue' and 'parole'. Langue refers to the system of language, the rules and conventions which organise it. This is language as a social institution. Parole refers to the individual utterance, the individual use of language. To clarify this point, Saussure compares language to the game of chess. Here, we can distinguish between the rules of the game and an actual game of chess. Without the body of rules ('langue') there could be no actual game, but it is only in an actual game ('parole') that these rules are made manifest. It is the homogeneity of the structure which makes the heterogeneity of the performance possible.

Structuralism, as a mode of cultural analysis, takes two basic ideas from Saussure's work. First, a concern with the underlying relations of cultural texts and practices – the 'grammar' which makes meaning possible. Second, the view that meaning is always the result of the interplay of relationships of selection and combination made possible by the underlying structure. In other words, cultural texts and practices are studied as analogous to language. It is the underlying rules of cultural texts and practices which interest structuralists. It is structure which makes meaning possible. The task of structuralism, therefore, is to make explicit the rules and conventions ('langue') which govern the production of meaning(s) ('parole').

In his analysis of 'primitive' myth, the French anthropologist Claude Levi-Strauss (1968) claims that beneath the vast heterogeneity of myths there can be discovered a homogeneous structure. In other words, myths work like language. Seen in this way, the anthropologist's task is to discover the underlying 'grammar' – the rules and regulations which make it possible for myths to be meaningful. He argues that myths are structured in terms of 'binary oppositions'. Meaning is produced by dividing the world into mutually exclusive categories: culture/nature, man/woman, black/white, good/bad, us/them, etc.

According to Levi-Strauss, all myths have a similar socio-cultural function within society. Their purpose is to make the world explicable, to magically resolve its problems and contradictions. As he contends, 'mythical thought always progresses from the awareness of oppositions toward their resolution. . . . the purpose of myth is to provide a logical model capable of overcoming a contradiction' (1968: 224, 228). From this perspective, myths are stories we tell ourselves as a culture in order to banish contradictions and make the world explicable and therefore habitable.

In *Sixguns and Society*, Will Wright (1975) uses the methodology of structuralism (drawing on both Saussure and Levi-Strauss) to analyse the Hollywood Western as myth. His general aim is 'to show how the myths of a society, through their structure, communicate a conceptual order to the members of that society' (17). In particular, he seeks to demonstrate how the Western 'presents a symbolically simple but remarkably deep conceptualization of American social beliefs' (23).

According to Wright, the Western has evolved through three stages: 'classic' (including a variation he calls 'vengeance'), 'transition theme' and 'professional'. Despite the genre's different types, Wright identifies a basic set of structuring oppositions:

inside society	outside society
good	bad
strong	weak
civilization	wilderness (49)

But, as Wright insists (taking him beyond Levi-Strauss), in order to fully understand the social meaning of a myth, it is necessary to analyse not only its binary structure but also its narrative structure – the progression of events and the resolution of conflicts' (24). The 'classic' Western is divided into sixteen narrative 'functions':

1. The hero enters a social group.

2. The hero is unknown to the society.

3. The hero is revealed to have an exceptional ability.

4. The society recognises a difference between themselves and the hero; the hero is given a special status.

5. The society does not completely accept the hero.

6. There is a conflict of interests between the villains and the society.

7. The villains are stronger than the society; the society is weak.

8. There is a strong friendship or respect between the hero and a villain.

9. The villains threaten the society.

10. The hero avoids involvement in the conflict.

11. The villains endanger a friend of the hero.

12. The hero fights the villains.

13. The hero defeats the villains.

14. The society is safe.

15. The society accepts the hero.

16. The hero loses or gives up his special status. (48–9)

In the classic Western, the hero and society are (temporarily) aligned in opposition to the villains, who remain outside society. In the 'transition theme' Western, those that Wright claims provide a bridge between the classic Western, the form which dominated the 1930s, the 1940s and most of the 1950s, and the professional Western, the form which dominated the 1960s and 1970s, the binary oppositions are reversed, and we see the hero outside society struggling against a strong, but corrupt and corrupting, civilisation:

hero	society
outside society	inside society
good	bad
weak	strong
wilderness	civilization (165)

Many of the narrative functions are also inverted. Instead of being outside the society, the hero begins as a valued member of the society. But the society is revealed to be the real 'villain' in opposition to the hero and those outside society and civilisation. In his support for, and eventual alignment with, those outside society and civilisation, he himself crosses from inside to outside and from civilisation to wilderness. But in the end the society is too strong for those outside it, who are ultimately powerless against its force. The best they can do is escape to the wilderness.

In a rather reductive correspondence theory (which undermines much of the strength of Wright's approach), he claims that each type of Western 'corresponds' to a different moment in the recent economic development of the USA: 'the classic Western plot corresponds to the individualistic conception of society underlying a market economy. . . . [t]he vengeance plot is a variation that begins to reflect changes in the market economy. . . . [t]he professional plot reveals a new conception of society corresponding to the values and attitudes inherent in a planned, corporate economy' (15). Each type in turn articulates its own mythic version of how to achieve the *American Dream*:

> [t]he classical plot shows that the way to achieve such human rewards as friendship, respect, and dignity is to separate yourself from others and use your strength as an autonomous individual to succor them. . . . The vengeance variation . . . weakens the compatibility of the individual and society by showing that the path to respect

and love is to separate yourself from others, struggling individually against your many and strong enemies but striving to remember and return to the softer values of marriage and humility. The transition theme, anticipating new social values, argues that love and companionship are available – at the cost of becoming a social outcast – to the individual who stands firmly and righteously against the intolerance and ignorance of society. Finally, the professional plot . . . argues that companionship and respect are to be achieved only by becoming a skilled technician, who joins an elite group of professionals, accepts any job that is offered, and has loyalty only to the integrity of the team, not to any competing social or community values. (186–7)

POSTSTRUCTURALISM AND POPULAR FILM

Poststructuralists reject the idea of an underlying structure ultimately determining the meaning of a cultural text or practice. For poststructuralists, meaning is always in process, a momentary stop in a continuous flow of possibilities. Whereas Saussure posited language as consisting of the relationship between the signifier, signified and sign, the theorists of poststructuralism contend that the situation is more complex than this. Signifiers do not produce signifieds, they produce more signifiers. Meaning as a result is a very unstable thing, always in a sense both present and absent. Jacques Derrida (1973) has invented a new word to describe the divided nature of the sign: 'différance', meaning both to defer and to differ. The sign, as we have noted, is made meaningful for Saussure by being different. Derrida adds to this the notion that meaning is also always deferred, never fully present, always both absent and present. For example, if we track the meaning of a word through a dictionary, we encounter a relentless deferment of meaning, as one signifier produces a signified, which in turn becomes another signifier. Tracking through the dictionary in this way confirms a relentless intertextual deferment of meaning, 'the indefinite referral of signifier to signifier . . . which gives the signified meaning no respite . . . so that it always signifies again' (Derrida 1978: 25). It is only when located in a discourse and read in a context that there is a temporary halt to the endless play of signifier to signifier. If, for example, I read or hear the words 'leaving Las Vegas', they would mean something quite different depending on whether they were the opening words of a novel, a line from a poem, an excuse, a jotting in a traveller's notebook, a line from a song, an example from a phrasebook, a metaphor for bringing to an end a hopeless commitment, a roadside sign, part of a monologue in a play, part of a speech in a film, an illustration in an explanation of 'différance'. But even discourse and context cannot fully control meaning: the phrase 'leaving Las Vegas' will carry with it the 'trace' of meanings from other contexts. If I know that the line is from a song (of the same title by Sheryl Crow), this will resonate across the words as I read them on a roadside sign.

Jacques Lacan's poststructuralist account of the development of the subject has had an enormous influence on both cultural studies and film studies. Lacan takes Freud's developmental structure and rearticulates it through a critical reading of structuralism to produce a poststructuralist psychoanalysis. According to Lacan, we make a journey through three determinate stages of development. The first stage is the 'mirror phase'; the second is the 'fort–da' game, and the third is the 'Oedipus complex'. In the mythical moment of plenitude, there is no clear distinction between subject and object. Our union with the mother is perfect and complete. This is followed by a period experienced as one of 'fragmentation': beyond the constant satisfactions of the womb, now dependent on the intermittent satisfactions of the breast. A sense of self to challenge the experience of fragmentation, and promise control over our own needs, emerges during what Lacan calls the 'mirror phase'. Looking in the mirror (real or imagined), we begin to construct a sense of self. The mirror phase is the moment (supposedly between the ages of six and eighteen months) when we first recognise ourselves in a mirror. On the basis of this recognition or, more properly, *misrecognition* (not the self, but an image of the self), we begin to see ourselves as separate individuals; that

61

is, we see ourselves as more complete, more unified than our physical development actually exhibits. The mirror phase heralds the moment of entry into an order of subjectivity which Lacan calls the imaginary:

> [t]he imaginary for Lacan is precisely this realm of *images* in which we make identifications, but in the very act of doing so are led to misperceive and misrecognize ourselves. As a child grows up, it will continue to make such imaginary identifications with objects, and this is how the ego will be built up. For Lacan, the ego is just this narcissistic process whereby we bolster up a fictive sense of unitary selfhood by finding something in the world with which we can identify (Eagleton 1983: 165)

With each new image, we will attempt to return to a time before 'lack', to find ourselves in what is not ourselves; and each time we will fail.

The second stage of development, the 'fort–da' game, originally named by Freud after watching his grandson throw a cotton reel away ('gone') and then pull it back again ('here') by means of an attached thread. Freud saw this as the child's way of coming to terms with its mother's absence – the reel symbolically representing the mother, over which the child is exerting mastery. Lacan rereads this as a representation of the child's introduction *into* language. Through language, we enter what Lacan calls the symbolic. This is the order of culture. It is here that we acquire our human subjectivity. Language allows us to communicate with others, but it also intensifies our experience of 'lack'. Our demands can now be articulated through language, but they cannot make good our experience of 'lack' – they only intensify it. Our entry into language, and the symbolic, opens up a gap between our need for the original moment of plenitude and the promise and failure of language; it is in this gap that desire emerges. It is in and through language that the subject becomes a subject: subject in, subject of, and ultimately subject to, language. I can only be 'I' in and through language. But again there is a price to pay: Lacan distinguishes between the subject of the enunciation and the subject of the enounced. When 'I' speak, I am always different from the 'I' of whom I speak; always sliding into difference and defeat: 'when the subject appears somewhere as meaning, he is manifested elsewhere as "fading", as disappearance' (Lacan 1977a: 218). Subjectivity is thus produced from the very processes of language, made and remade within its patterns and articulations, and not an essential pre-given as 'rational' accounts presuppose. The symbolic order is something which pre-exists us: it is already there waiting for us to take our places. It produces our very subjectivity and yet it is forever outside our sense of being, belonging to others in the same way as it belongs to us. I am 'I' when I speak to you and 'you' when you speak to me. It follows from this that our sense of being a unique individual is somewhat fragile. In other words, there can be no such thing as an essential self. It is nothing more than a fiction we live by. Not only does the language we speak produce our subjectivity, we are subjects of its structural processes. But more than this, Lacan insists that our unconscious is also constructed out of our contact with language. In other words, our sense of self and our sense of otherness are both composed from the language we speak and the cultural repertoire we encounter in our everyday existence. It is language which enables us to think ourselves as subjects: without language we would have no sense of self, and yet within language our sense of self is always slipping away – fragile and threatening to fragment.

The third stage of development is the Oedipus complex: the encounter with sexual difference. In a classic structuralist move, Lacan rewrites the Oedipus complex in terms of language. The unconscious is itself structured like a language. What takes him beyond structuralism is his account of desire. The Oedipal movement from the imaginary to the symbolic leaves the child moving from one signifier to another. Desire itself is the process or pursuit of the fixed signified (the 'other', the 'real'), always forever becoming another signifier – the 'incessant sliding of the signified under the signifier' (Lacan 1977b: 154). Desire is the impossibility of closing the gap between self and other – to make good that which we 'lack'. The 'lesson' of the Oedipus complex is that

> [t]he child must now resign itself to the fact that it can never have any *direct* access to reality, in particular to the prohibited body of the mother. It has been banished from this 'full', imaginary possession into the 'empty' world of language . . . the 'metaphorical' world of the mirror has yielded ground to the 'metonymic' world of language. . . . This potentially endless movement from one signifier to another is what Lacan means by desire. All desire springs from a lack, which it strives continually to fill . . . To enter language is to be severed from what Lacan calls the 'real', that inaccessible realm which is always beyond the reach of signification, always outside the symbolic order. In particular, we are severed from the mother's body: after the Oedipus crisis, we will never again be able to attain this precious object, even though we will spend all our lives hunting for it. We have to make do instead with substitute objects . . . with which we try vainly to plug the gap at the very centre of our being. We move among substitutes for substitutes, metaphors for metaphors, never able to recover the pure (if fictive) self-identity and self-completion which we knew in the imaginary. . . . In Lacanian theory, it is an original lost object – the mother's body – which drives forward the narrative of our lives, impelling us to pursue substitutes for this lost paradise in the endless metonymic movement of desire. (Eagleton 1983: 167, 168, 185)

According to Lacan, then, we are born into a condition of 'lack', and subsequently spend the rest of our lives trying to overcome this condition. 'Lack' is experienced in different ways and as different things, but it is always a non-representable expression of the fundamental condition of 'lack'. As we move forward, we are driven by a desire to overcome the condition, and as we look back we continue to believe that the union with the mother was a moment of plenitude before the fall into 'lack'. The result is an endless quest in research of an imagined moment of plenitude. Lacan figures this as a search for what he terms *l'objet petit a*:

an endless quest for a non-existent object, signifying an imaginary moment in time. We console ourselves with a series of substitutes for a substitute (see chapter 7 below for discussion in relation to theories of consumption).

Laura Mulvey's (1975) work is in part an attempt to appropriate the poststructuralist psychoanalysis of Lacan for a feminist film criticism. Using Lacan, she constructs an analysis of how popular cinema produces and reproduces what she calls the 'male gaze'. The inscription of the image of women in this system is twofold: she is the object of a male desire, and she is the signifier of the threat of castration.

Mulvey's argument is that popular cinema produces two contradictory forms of visual pleasure. First, there is scopophilia, the pleasure of looking: 'taking other people as objects, subjecting them to a controlling gaze' (8). The notion of the controlling gaze is crucial to Mulvey's argument. But so is sexual objectification: scopophilia is also sexual, 'using another person as an object of sexual stimulation through sight' (10). Although it clearly presents itself to be seen, Mulvey argues that the conventions of popular cinema are such as to suggest a 'hermetically sealed world which unwinds magically, indifferent to the presence of the audience' (9). The audiences' 'voyeuristic phantasy' is encouraged by the contrast between the darkness of the cinema and the changing patterns of light on the screen.

Popular cinema promotes and satisfies a second pleasure; 'developing scopophilia in its narcissistic aspect' (9). Here, Mulvey draws on Lacan's account of the mirror phase to suggest that there is an analogy to be made between the constitution of a child's ego and the pleasures of cinematic identification. Just as a child recognises and misrecognises itself in the mirror, the spectator recognises and misrecognises itself on the screen.

In a world structured by 'sexual imbalance', the pleasure of the gaze has been separated into two distinct positions: men look and women exhibit '*to-be-looked-at-ness*' – both playing to and signifying male desire (11). Women are therefore crucial to the pleasure of the (male) gaze. 'Traditionally, the woman displayed has functioned on two levels: as erotic object for the characters within the screen story, and as erotic object for the spectator within the auditorium, with a shifting tension between the looks on either side of the screen' (11–12). She gives the example of the showgirl who can be seen to dance for both looks. When the heroine removes her clothes, it is for the sexual gaze of both the hero in the narrative and the spectator in the auditorium. It is only when they subsequently make love that a tension arises between the two looks.

Popular cinema is structured around two moments: moments of narrative and moments of spectacle. The first is associated with the active male, the second with the passive female. The male spectator fixes his gaze on the hero ('the bearer of the look') to satisfy libido. The first look recalls the moment of recognition/misrecognition in front of the mirror. The second look confirms women as sexual objects. The second look is made more complex by the claim that

> [u]ltimately, the meaning of woman is sexual difference . . . She connotes something that the look continually circles around but disavows: her lack of a penis, implying a threat of castration and hence unpleasure. . . . Thus the woman as icon, displayed for the gaze and enjoyment of men, the active controllers of the look, always threatens to evoke the anxiety it originally signified. (13)

To salvage pleasure and escape an unpleasurable re-enactment of the original castration complex, the male unconscious can take two routes to safety. The first means of escape is through detailed investigation of the original moment of trauma, usually leading to 'the devaluation, punishment or saving of the guilty object' (13). Mulvey cites the narratives of film noir as typical of this method of anxiety-control. The second means of escape is through 'complete disavowal of castration by the substitution of a fetish object or turning the represented figure itself into a fetish so that it becomes reassuring rather than dangerous' (13–14). Mulvey cites 'the cult of the female star . . . [in which] fetishistic scopophilia builds up the physical beauty of the object, transforming it into something satisfying in itself' (14). This often leads to the erotic look of the spectator no longer being borne by the look of the male protagonist, producing moments of pure erotic spectacle as the camera holds the female body (often fragmented) for the unmediated erotic look of the spectator.

Mulvey concludes her argument by suggesting that the pleasure of popular cinema must be destroyed in order to liberate women from the exploitation and oppression of being the '(passive) raw material for the (active) male gaze' (17). To produce a cinema no longer 'obsessively subordinated to the neurotic needs of the male ego' (18), it is necessary to break with illusionism, making the camera material, and producing in the audience 'dialectics, passionate detachment' (18). Moreover, '[w]omen, whose image has continually been stolen and used for this end [objects of the male gaze], cannot view the decline of the traditional film form with anything much more than sentimental regret' (18).

Mulvey's influence has been enormous. However, some feminists and others working within film and cultural studies have begun to doubt its 'universal validity' (Gamman and Marshment 1988: 5), questioning whether 'the gaze is always male, or whether it is "merely dominant" ' among a range of different ways of seeing, including the female gaze (5). A particular problem for cultural studies is Mulvey's account of the audience as purely textual – a homogenous and passive production of the text. There is no room in Mulvey's theory for social, historical subjects who arrive at the cinema with a range of competing and contradictory discourses, which confront and 'negotiate' with the discourses of the film. As Lisa Taylor (1995) notes, 'It is vital to recognise that women are not simply the passive objects of a monolithic 'patriarchal ideology', but are actively engaged in resistances and struggles within their everyday lives' (167).

CULTURAL STUDIES AND POPULAR FILM

Writing in the late 1980s, Christine Gledhill notes 'the recent renewal of feminist interest in mainstream popular culture' (1988: 241). As she also points out, it is a renewal largely happening in opposition to 'the ideological analysis of the late 1970s and early 1980s, influenced by poststructuralism and cine-psychoanalysis, [which] rejected mainstream cinema for its production of patriarchal/bourgeois spectatorship and simultaneous repression of femininity' (24). Rather than the spectator produced by the text, it is interested in 'the conditions of . . . consumption in the lives of sociohistorically constituted audiences' (241). In a Gramscian move, Gledhill advocates an understanding of the relationship between spectators and film text as one of 'negotiation'.

> The value of this notion lies in its avoidance of an overly deterministic view of cultural production, whether economistic (the media product reflects dominant economic interests outside the text), or cine-psychoanalytic (the text constructs spectators through the psycholinguistic mechanisms of the patriarchal Unconscious). For the term 'negotiation' implies the holding together of opposite sides in an ongoing process of give-and-take. As a model of meaning production, negotiation conceives cultural exchange as the intersection of processes of production and reception, in which overlapping but non-matching determinations operate. Meaning is neither imposed, nor passively imbibed, but arises out of a struggle or negotiation between competing frames of reference, motivation and experience. (244)

Gledhill suggests that negotiation can be analysed at three different levels: audiences, texts, institutions. Reception 'is potentially the most radical moment of negotiation, because the most variable and unpredictable' (246). As she points out, 'The viewing or reading situation affects the meanings and pleasures of a work by introducing into the cultural exchange a range of determinations, potentially resistant or contradictory, arising from the differential social and cultural constitution of readers or viewers – by class, gender, race, age, personal history, and so on' (246).

Based on research carried out at the end of the 1980s, Jackie Stacey (1994) develops and elaborates this approach. Like Gledhill, Stacey seeks to go beyond the textual determinism which places women spectators as the passive consumers of the male gaze. She rejects 'the universalism of much psychoanalytic work on female spectatorship' (14). Rather than drawing her conclusions from an analysis solely of the film text itself, she explores instead the processes and practices of actual women consuming film. The question which she poses is how women make sense of what they see and do at the cinema. The specific focus of her study is the relationship in the 1940s and 1950s between Hollywood female film stars and British female spectators. She is determined to take 'the audience seriously in an attempt to counter both the popular and, indeed, the critical assumption that audiences (especially female ones!) are "passive dupes" who are easily manipulated by the media' (12).

In particular, she challenges psychoanalytic criticism's account of female spectatorship as little more than an effect of filmic discourse, a position and a site produced and addressed by the discourse of film (see the discussion of Laura Mulvey above). Her study seeks to go beyond the 'textual spectator' to analyse the responses of actual women in the audience. To do this, she finds it necessary to step outside the paradigm of film studies and embrace instead the concerns of cultural studies. Here is her useful diagram of the contrasting paradigms of film studies and cultural studies (24):

Film studies	Cultural studies
Spectatorship positioning	Audience readings
Textual analysis	Ethnographic methods
Meaning as production-led	Meaning as consumption-led
Passive viewer	Active viewer
Unconscious	Conscious
Pessimistic	Optimistic

Stacey's findings are based on research which she carried out on a group of British white women, mostly aged over 60, and mostly working-class, who responded to an advertisement which she placed in two women's magazines, *Woman's Realm* and *Woman's Weekly*, asking for women to reply if they were keen cinema-goers in the 1940s and 1950s. Those who replied (350) were asked to complete a questionnaire (238 complied). She organised her analysis of their letters and completed questionnaires in terms of three discourses generated by the responses themselves: 'escapism', 'identification' and 'consumerism'.

The term 'escapism' is most often used pejoratively, applied to popular culture in order to condemn it as trivial and unworthy of critical or academic engagement. 'Indeed', as she points out, 'this has been particularly true of forms of popular culture enjoyed by women' (90). However, her findings tend to problematise this easy dismissal – suggesting the multi-dimensional nature of the 'escapism' of cinema-going in the 1940s and 1950s. 'Escapism' is one of the most frequently-cited reasons given by her respondents for going to the cinema. Using Richard Dyer's (1981) argument for the utopian sensibility of popular entertainment, Stacey constructs an account of the utopian possibilities of Hollywood cinema for her female respondents. Dyer argues that entertainment's utopian sensibility is best understood in terms of a series of binary oppositions between problems experienced by the would-be audience and solutions to these problems played out in the texts and practices of entertainment.

Social problems	Textual solutions
scarcity	abundance
exhaustion	energy
dreariness	intensity
manipulation	transparency
fragmentation	community

However, whereas for Dyer entertainment's utopian sensibility is a property played out in the text or practice, Stacey extends his argument to take into account the total experience of going to the cinema. An analysis of her respondents' letters and answers to her questionnaire make it clear that the pleasures of the cinema were always more than the visual pleasures of the cinema text. She found that besides the obvious appeal of the glamour of the Hollywood stars, other less obvious pleasures included the ritual of attending a screening, the shared experience and community of the audience, the comfort and comparative luxury of the cinema itself. Moreover, each pleasure sustained and secured the others.

> Associated as it was with luxury and glamour, in contrast to British drabness at this time, Hollywood was remembered

as offering an escape to a materially better world. Thus the specific association of the luxury of Hollywood with the luxury of the cinema interiors at this time clearly contributed to the multi-layered meanings of escapism for female spectators. (97)

In addition, as she points out,

> The physical space of the cinema provided a transitional space between everyday life outside the cinema and the fantasy world of the Hollywood film about to be shown. Its design and decor facilitated the processes of escapism enjoyed by these female spectators. As such, cinemas were dream palaces not only in so far as they housed the screening of Hollywood fantasies, but also because of their design and decor which provided a feminised and glamorised space suitable for the cultural consumption of Hollywood films. (99)

She quite rightly insists on the historical specificity of her respondents' escapism. They are not only escaping *into* the luxury of the cinema and the glamour of Hollywood film, they are also escaping *from* the hardships, dangers and restrictions of wartime Britain.

Stacey's second focus is 'identification', 'the relationship between stars and spectators and the processes of the formation of feminine identities through cinematic modes of address' (126). The spectator knows she is not the star, yet for the duration of the film there is a 'temporary fluidity' (126) between her identity and the identity of the Hollywood star. The temporary fluidity was often triggered by a sense of similarity (something shared – hair-colouring, for example). As Stacey explains, 'on the one hand, they value difference for taking them into a world in which their desires could potentially be fulfilled; on the other, they value similarity for enabling them to recognise qualities they already have' (128). Often, identification would extend beyond the cinema to produce what Stacey calls 'identifactory practices' (as distinguished from 'identifactory fantasies'), imitating behaviour and copying appearances.

Stacey is aware that identification is often the key term in claims about female spectatorship made in terms of collusion and complicity. In such analysis, identification is theorised as the successful positioning of the female spectator (as either passive or masochistic) in the interests of patriarchy. However, shifting the focus from the film text to actual spectators in the audience, she finds that the concept of identification undergoes something of a sea change. Although stars may have an ideological function, in that they act as role models in the circulation of normative models of feminine beauty and sexual attractiveness, this is by no means the whole story. Stacey's respondents continually draw attention to the way in which stars can generate fantasies of power, control and self-confidence. 'Hollywood stars can thus be seen as offering more than simple role models of sexual attractiveness (though clearly they offer this too!). However, they were also remembered as offering female spectators a source of fantasy of a more powerful and confident self' (158).

Stacey's final move is to analyse the ways in which her respondents related to Hollywood stars in terms of 'consumption'. Again, she rejects the monolithic assumptions of previous approaches which assume that, in the final analysis, consumption is always successfully located in a relationship of domination, control and exploitation. Without discounting the commodity tie-ins (especially fashion and cosmetics) which formed part of the cinema-going experience (even in the 1940s and 1950s, and how these might give rise to an analysis which theorised consumption as pandering to the male gaze and facilitating the reproduction of consumer capitalism, Stacey argues for an account which takes seriously 'women's agency as consumers and highlights the contradictions of consumption for women' (185). She insists that 'consumption is a site of negotiated meanings, of resistance and of appropriation as well as of subjection and exploitation' (187).

According to Stacey, 'film studies work on consumption has tended to perpetuate a very production-led approach to the subject, (taking) as its object of study the ways in which the film industry produces cinema spectators as consumers of both the film and the products of other industries' (188). Focusing too exclusively on production, analysis is never able to pose theoretically (let alone discuss in concrete detail) how audiences use and make meanings from the commodities which they consume. She argues that her respondents' accounts of consumption in the 1940s and 1950s 'highlight a more contradictory relationship between spectatorship and consumption than that presented by the production studies' (190). For example, she notes the ways in which 'American feminine ideals are clearly remembered as transgressing restrictive British femininity and thus employed as strategies of resistance' (198). 'Hollywood stars represented fashions on the screen which were identified by spectators as transgressing restrictive codes of British feminine appearance' (204). Thus the consumption of Hollywood stars and the commodities associated with them was a means to negotiate with and extend notions of British femininity. Many of the letters and completed questionnaires point to the way in which the Hollywood stars represented an alternative femininity, exciting and transgressive. As she explains,

> As well as being vehicles to encourage female spectators to become consumers, and to improve their appearances . . . Hollywood stars were also contested terrains of competing cultural discourses of femininity . . . [T]hey were central to challenges to what was perceived as restrictive British femininity. (205)

Stacey does not argue that these women were free to determine their feminine identifies through acts of consumption. But she does insist on 'the importance of maintaining a theoretical understanding of the space between dominant discourses of consumption and female spectators' consumer practices in different locations' (218). Nor does she deny that such forms of consumption may pander to the patriarchal gaze. But she does insist that 'the consumption of Hollywood stars and other commodities for the transformation of self-image produces something in excess of the needs of dominant culture' (223). She contends that

> Paradoxically, whilst commodity consumption for female spectators in mid to late 1950s Britain concerns producing oneself as a desirable object, it also offers an escape from what is perceived as the drudgery of domesticity and motherhood which increasingly comes to define femininity at this time.

> Thus, consumption may signify an assertion of self in opposition to the self-sacrifice associated with marriage and motherhood in 1950s Britain. (238).

She concludes that her respondents' accounts of Hollywood stars point to the possibility of 'the use of *American* femininity to rebel against what they perceived as restrictive *British* norms (238). Moreover, she argues, 'The production of a feminine self in relation to Americanness signified 'autonomy', 'individuality' and 'independence' to many female spectators in Britain at this time' (238).

Stacey's approach represents an excellent counter to the universalistic claims of much cine-psychoanalysis. Moving analysis, as she does, from the film text to the female audience, Hollywood's patriarchal power begins to look less monolithic, less seamless. By studying the female audience, 'female spectatorship might be seen as a process of negotiating the dominant meanings of Hollywood cinema, rather than one of being passively positioned by it' (12).

5

NEWSPAPERS
AND MAGAZINES

THE POPULAR PRESS

To understand the popular press as popular culture, I think we must learn, from the Norwegian critic Jostein Gripsrud (1992), 'to transcend the futile moralism frequently present in critiques of it'. This does not mean that we must ' "defend" the popular press in any simplistic populist or "anti-elitist" manner, but suggests an understanding of it which differs from the usual lamentations about "commercialism", "vulgarity", etc.' (84).

What are the connections to be made between tabloid journalism and popular culture? Peter Dahlgren (1992) suggests that one 'key link' is storytelling. He sees storytelling as one of the two basic modes of knowing and making sense of the world, the other being the analytic mode. The analytic mode is marked by 'referential information and logic'; the storytelling mode by 'the narratological configurations which provide coherence via enplotment' (14). The official aim of journalism is to present information about the world and is thus a commitment to the analytic mode. However, in practice, it is the storytelling mode which is most often brought into play. Moreover, Dahlgren insists that this is not another way of distinguishing 'between serious and tabloid news, between fact and fiction'; there is between both a 'storytelling continuum' (15).

For Colin Sparks (1992), the key difference between the popular press and the so-called 'quality' press is the mobilisation (by the popular press) of the 'personal' as an explanatory framework. In an analysis of news values, he found that even when the stories in the popular press and the 'quality press' are the same, they are always treated differently.

> [Whereas the] 'quality' press presents 'a fragmented picture of the world in which the construction of coherence and totality is the work of the reader, the popular press embeds a form of immediacy and totality in its handling of public issues. In particular, this immediacy of explanation is achieved by means of a direct appeal to personal experience. The popular conception of the personal becomes the explanatory framework within which the social order is presented as transparent. (39)

Sparks illustrates his point in a comparison of the respective coverage by *The Sun* and *The Times* of the prison riot in Strangeways jail in April 1990. Although the personal is present in *The Times*'s coverage of the riot, it is not used as the explanatory framework. Instead, the paper attempts to locate the riot 'within a framework which contained different kinds of information and knowledge' (40). The reader is invited, more or less, to make sense of an ongoing series of events. *The Sun*, on the other hand, explained events in 'an immediate explanatory framework in terms of individual and personal causes and responses' (40). Whereas *The Times* presented a range of resources from which to make sense of an event with a past, present and future, *The Sun* reduced the timescale to an unchanging *Now*, in which certain prisoners did this because other prisoners did that. Although Sparks acknowledges the possibility of 'popular productivity' reworking the meanings presented by *The Sun*, he concludes that 'it seems to me that this is so massively determined a discourse of the "reactionary popular" that it is impossible to rescue it for any conception of progress' (41). The best that can be claimed for the politics of the popular press is that it can 'mobilize a certain ill-defined discontent'. Although it may 'speak in an idiom recognizable by the masses as more or less related to their own [it can] only speak of their concerns, joys and discontents within the limits set for it by the existing structures of society' (28).

John Fiske's approach to the popular press is located in the general claim that 'popular culture is potentially, and often actually, progressive (though not radical)' (1989a: 21). He explains the distinction between progressive and radical as follows: '[p]opular texts may be progressive in that they can encourage the production of meanings that work to change or destabilize the social order, but they can never be radical in the sense that they can never oppose head on or overthrow that order' (133).

Fiske distinguishes the popular press from, on the one hand, the official press and, on the other, the alternative press. The popular press is, as he notes, despised by both. According to Fiske, the popular press operates on the borderline between the public and the private: 'its style is sensational, sometimes sceptical, sometimes moralistically earnest; its tone is populist; its modality fluidly denies any stylistic difference between fiction and documentary, between news and entertainment' (1992a: 48).

Fiske's analysis of the popular press begins from Stuart Hall's (in Storey 1994) claim that the central political division in late capitalist societies is the opposition: '[t]he people versus the power-bloc' (465). The 'power-bloc' is a shifting alliance of the forces of domination, expressed in and through institutions such as the media, the culture industries, government, the educational system, etc. 'The people' are also a shifting alliance, defined always in historically specific opposition to the 'power-bloc'. According to Fiske, the official press articulates the interests of the power-bloc in a top-down flow of information. 'A top-down definition of information is', he contends, 'a disciplinary one, and it hides its disciplinarity under notions of objectivity, responsibility and political education. What the people ought to know for a liberal democracy to function properly is a concept that hides repression under its liberal rhetoric and power under its pluralism' (1992a: 49). In other words, the official press, according to Fiske, provide the information and knowledge necessary to ensure the maintenance of the prevailing structures of power. But more than this, it produces what he calls a 'believing subject' (49). This is for Fiske one of the key differences between the official and the popular press.

> The last thing that tabloid journalism produces is a believing subject. One of its most characteristic tones of voice is that of a sceptical laughter which offers the pleasures of disbelief, the pleasures of not being taken in. This popular pleasure of 'seeing through' them (whoever constitutes the powerful *them* of the moment) is the historical result of centuries of subordination which the people have not allowed to develop into subjection. (49)

Fiske uses an example a recurrent story in the American popular press, that of aliens from space. What interests Fiske is not the main story but its frequent subtheme, that the evidence for the existence of aliens from space and the evidence of UFO landings is being covered up by both the American and Russian governments. What is important here, according to Fiske, is not whether space aliens have or have not actually landed; 'what is at stake is the opposition between popular knowledge and power-bloc knowledge – and it is the opposition, not the knowledge itself, that matters' (49). Fiske contends that such stories stage a 'utopian' assault on the 'normalization' which is essential for the smooth operation of the disciplinary procedures of the power-bloc. The popular press is full of utopian fantasies of another way of understanding the world which challenges the normalising 'reality' of the power-bloc. The popular press produces the sceptical subject who hovers between belief and disbelief, playing thoughtfully in the unresolved contradictions. As Fiske explains, 'recognizing this requires us to view the people as social agents rather than social subjects. The multiplicity of contradictions and their lack of resolution debars any of the coherence necessary to produce and position unified or even divided subjectivities: instead they require active social agents to negotiate them' (53). In effect, what Fiske does is to reverse the claim made by Sparks about the textual difference between 'quality' and popular press. Moreover, the popular press,

> unlike its official counterpart, makes no effort to present its information to us as an objective set of facts in an unchanging

universe: for it, information is not an essentialist knowledge system but is a process that works only in a political relationship to other knowledges. Its politics lies in its oppositionality to the normal, the official. (54)

A key issue for Fiske is relevance. Relevance is not something that can be dictated from above, it is always a production from below. The official press, according to Fiske, using a term from Michel de Certeau (1984), operates with a

> 'scriptural economy' which attempts to discipline its readers into 'deciphering' its texts rather than 'reading' them. Deciphering a text is subjecting oneself to its truth . . . reading, however, involves bringing to the text oral competencies developed in the immediate conditions of the reader's social history. Reading is thus a negotiation (typically for de Certeau an antagonistic one) between a text produced from the top and its reading from below. Unresolved contradictions, unstable, unfinished knowledge, scepticism, parody and excess all invite reading: truth and objectivity invite decipherment. Reading is participatory, it involves the production of relevance; decipherment, the perception and acceptance of distance (social and aesthetic). (59)

For the press, popular or otherwise, to become popular culture it has to be taken up by 'the people'; it must provoke conversation and enter oral circulation and recirculation. As he explains it, 'Top-down, or official news [for example], has to be re-informed by popular productivity if it is to be made relevant to everyday life' (57). In the final analysis, it is popular productivity which transforms the popular press into popular culture. Like everything else made available by the media and culture industries, it has to be *made* popular.

Ian Connell (1992) takes up a position similar to the one advocated by Fiske. He argues that the popular press, what he calls its 'fantastical reportage', 'sustain[s] certain justifiable resentments' (64). Fantastical or fabulous reportage (as Connell also calls it) does not produce resistance in the form suggested by

Fiske. General discontent mingles with the particular as fantastical reportage 'fuels their resentment of superordinates and all they possess' (66). Rather than reading in resentment against the power-bloc, Connell maintains that

> Readers engaged by the stories . . . probably want instead all the rewards that [the power-bloc] have granted the fallen heroes of these stories. The main characters of the stories they read have gained, by means made to seem questionable, all the trappings of a good life to which at best they have limited access. I suspect readers recognize the life depicted as good, but desire rather than reject what it can offer. What they are opposed to is their exclusion from it. (66)

Connell argues that media and cultural studies has failed to understand or explain this kind of oppositional resentment. Stories of the rich and famous falling from grace are the stock-in-trade of the popular press.

> Above all what these stories do is mount a populist challenge on privilege. . . . While the stories articulate neither a coherent political philosophy nor strategy, their splenetic outbursts do have, however, important political impact. What these stories do is bash the 'power-bloc' – or those representatives of it whose attributes and actions can be most meaningfully represented for their readers. (74)

The 'personalities' of these stories are presented 'as members of a *privileged* caste' (78). Time after time, the details of their wealth and their privileged lifestyles are paraded before the reader. Always mingled in the general narrative of misdeeds is the suggestion that they do not deserve their wealth and privilege. Connell's argument is that the popular press and its readers share a moral economy, a particular set of assumptions about fame: 'It is a status which grants rewards, but it also grants certain responsibilities' (81). This is a morality concerned with the uses and abuses of power and privilege. But, as Connell insists, moral disapprobation is not the main function of these stories. These are above all else

political stories in that they articulate relations of antagonism
between

1. powerful elites (from which are drawn the tragic heroes
   and heroines of the tales);

2. narrators who are by a variety of means in touch with
   the goings-on of the elites, but who are not at one
   with them;

3. the rest of us, the powerless ordinary people on whose
   behalf the stories are told. (81)

The stories articulate a moral economy in which the world is divided
between those with power and privilege and those without power
and privilege (the 'haves' and the 'have-nots'). At times, there is
even the suggestion that those with privilege and power have it at
the expense of those without privilege and power. But this is not a
radical outrage. Although it offers the pleasure(s) of being a part
of an attack on power and privilege, ultimately its resentments are
conservative.

> They are not against privileges being granted, merely angry
> that they have been granted to the wrong people – to 'them'
> and not 'us', not to 'me'. Their mission is not so much to put
> a stop to gross inequalities as to redistribute them. Worse still
> perhaps is the possibility that the populism is a sham. The
> most vitriolic of the attacks seem to be reserved for those who
> by good fortune have found themselves one of the stars. They
> have not been born to stardom. It is, therefore, as if the tabloids
> are waiting for the inevitable, the moment when these parvenu
> personalities give themselves away and reveal the ordinariness
> of their origins. (82)

While Connell insists that this is the case, he also concedes that the
stories 'can and do undermine the authority of those who would
place themselves apart. They encourage and nourish scepticism
about the legitimacy of the class of personalities to act as they
do' (82).

MAGAZINES FOR WOMEN AND GIRLS

Angela McRobbie (1991), in an influential essay first published in 1978, argues that *Jackie*, the best-selling teenage girls' magazine in the 1970s, can be analysed 'as a system of messages, a signifying system and a bearer of a certain ideology, an ideology which deals with the construction of teenage femininity' (81–2). *Jackie*, together with other magazines for teenage girls, operates 'to win and shape the consent of the readers to a particular set of values' (82). Like other magazines for both girls and women, *Jackie* promotes 'a feminine culture' (83). Every stage from childhood to womanhood and old age is mapped out in terms of what is expected for the successful fulfilment of femininity. When reading *Jackie*, for example, 'teenage girls are subjected to an explicit attempt to win consent to the dominant order – in terms of femininity, leisure and consumption' (87).

McRobbie identifies four strategies ('subcodes') through which *Jackie* makes its appeal. These are:

1. the code of romance;

2. the code of personal/domestic life;

3. the code of fashion and beauty;

4. the code of pop music. (93)

The code of romance pervades almost every aspect of the magazine. Romance is defined as both serious and fun. 'At the "heart" of this world is the individual girl looking for romance' (98). She is alone and in competition with other girls also alone. Friends are always potential rivals. Happiness is the heterosexual couple. A happy end is a boy and girl together. A girl alone signifies failure. As McRobbie contends, *Jackie*'s code of romance is narrow and explicit:

1. the girl has to fight to *get* and *keep* her man;

2. she can *never* trust another woman unless she is old and 'hideous' in which case she does not appear in these stories anyway;

3. despite this, romance, and being a girl, are fun. (101)

This is a world in which girls must define themselves in terms of their relations with boys. Relationships, other than romantic heterosexual relationship, are not possible. Moreover, the code of romance dictates female passivity. Girls can of course follow the advice of magazines about make-up, dress, and how to act with boys. But true romance only comes to those who wait. To actively pursue romance (be a 'flirt') is to court inevitable failure.

The code of personal life introduced the darker realm of actuality in contrast to the colourful world of romance. Its principal home is the problem page. Here, as in the world of romance, girls are isolated. The problem page both responds to this isolation and supports and succours it. It is here that we encounter the ideology of the magazine at its most explicit. As McRobbie contends, 'It hammers home, on the last but one page, all those ideas and values prevalent in the other sections, but this time in unambiguous black and white' (111).

The fashion and beauty code encourages girls to see the use of dress and cosmetics as an essential part of being feminine – 'a full-time job demanding skill, patience and learning' (122). According to McRobbie, 'The message is clear. Appearance is of paramount importance to the girl, it should be designed to please both boyfriend and boss alike and threaten the authority of neither' (125).

The code of pop music is not about making music or even about developing an informed interest in pop music; 'the readers are presented, yet again, with another opportunity to indulge their emotions, but this time on the pop-star figure rather than the boyfriend' (126). Girls are invited to look and listen.

McRobbie concludes that *Jackie* functions to map and, ultimately, to limit the feminine sphere. Girls are told how to act and what others expect of them. Their happiness is defined in terms of romantic fulfilment with the right boy. Everything else – including the friendship of other girls – is either preparation for this or an obstacle to be overcome.

Writing in the 1990s, McRobbie (1994) welcomes the fading popularity of *Jackie*, and other magazines like it, and the emergence of new magazines for teenage girls (like *Just Seventeen* and *Mizz*), with an emphasis on fashion and pop music, and attitudes influenced by the success and circulation of feminist ideas.

> *Just Seventeen* has replaced *Jackie* as the top-selling magazine among a female readership aged approximately between 12 and 16. If we look closely at the magazine, it is immediately clear how different it is from its predecessor. Most strikingly, the girl is no longer the victim of romance. . . . She no longer distrusts all girls including her best friend because they represent a threat and might steal her 'fella'. . . . In fact she no longer exists because the narrative mode in which she appeared three or four times every week, i.e. the picture love-story, no longer exists. Romance is an absent category in *Just Seventeen*. There is love and there is sex and there are boys, but the conventionally coded meta-narrative of romance which . . . could only create a neurotically dependent female subject, has gone for good. (1994: 164)

Janice Winship (1987) argues that 'to simply dismiss women's magazines [is] to dismiss the lives of millions of women who read and enjoyed them each week' (xiii). She contends that a feminist cultural studies must be able to explore the dialectic of 'attraction and rejection' (xiii). As she explains:

> Many of the guises of femininity in women's magazines contribute to the secondary status from which we still desire to free ourselves. At the same time it is the dress of femininity which is both source of the pleasure of being a woman – and not a man – and in part the raw material for a feminist vision of the future. . . . Thus for feminists one important issue women's magazines can raise is how *do* we take over their feminine ground to create new untrammelled images of and for ourselves? (xiii–xiv)

Part of Winship's project is 'to explain the appeal of the magazine formula and to critically consider its limitations and potential for change' (8). Since their inception in the late eighteenth century, women's magazines have offered their readers a mixture of advice and entertainment. Regardless of politics, women's magazines continue to operate as survival manuals, providing their readers with practical advice on how to survive in a patriarchal culture. This might take the form of an explicit feminist politics, *Spare Rib*, for example, or stories of women triumphing over adversity, say, for example, in *Woman's Own*. The politics may be different, but the formula is much the same.

Women's magazines appeal to their readers by means of a combination of entertainment and useful advice. This appeal, according to Winship, is organised around a range of 'fictions'. These can be the visual fictions of advertisements, or items on fashion, cookery or family and home. They can also be actual fictions: romantic serials, five-minute stories, etc. Finally, there are the stories of the famous and reports of events in the lives of 'ordinary' women and men. Each in its different way attempts to draw the reader into the world of the magazine, and ultimately into a world of consumption. But pleasure is not totally dependent on purchase. Winship recalls how, one hot July, she gained enormous visual pleasure from a magazine advertisement, showing a woman diving into an ocean surreally continuous with the tap-end of a bath, without any intention of buying the product. She contends that we can 'recognise and relish the vocabulary of dreams in which ads deal' and we can 'vicariously indulge . . . in the fictions they create', while knowing all the time that their promises are probably false (56). Magazine advertisements, like the magazines themselves, provide a terrain on which to dream.

What is really being sold in the fictions of women's magazines, in editorials or advertisements, fashion and home-furnishing items, cookery and cosmetics, is successful and therefore *pleasurable* femininity. Follow *this* practical advice or buy *this* product and be a better lover, a better mother, a better wife, a better woman. The problem with all this from a feminist perspective is that it is always constructed around a mythical individual woman, existing outside, for example, powerful social and cultural structures and constraints.

Women's magazines also construct 'fictional collectivities' of women (67). This can be seen in the insistent 'we' of editorials; but it is also there in the reader–editor interactions of the letters page.

Here, we often find women making sense of the everyday world through a mixture of optimism and fatalism. Winship identifies this tension as an expression of women being 'ideologically bound to the personal terrain and in a position of relative powerlessness about public events' (70). Like the so-called 'triumph over tragedy' stories, the readers' letters and editorial responses often reveal a profound commitment to the 'individual solution'. Both 'teach' the same parable: individual effort will overcome all odds. The reader is interpellated as admiring subject, her own problems put in context; she is able to carry on. Short stories work in much the same way. What links these different 'fictions' is 'that the human triumphs they detail are emotional and not material ones' (76). In many ways, this is essential for the continued existence of the magazines' imagined communities; for to move from the emotional to the material is to run the risk of encountering the divisive presence of class and race.

> Thus the 'we women' feeling magazines construct is actually comprised of [sic] different cultural groups; the very notion of 'we' and 'our world', however, constantly undercuts those divisions to give the semblance of a unity – inside magazines. Outside, when the reader closes her magazine, she is no longer 'friends' with Esther Rantzen and her ilk; but while it lasted it has been a pleasant and reassuring dream. (77)

This is perhaps even more evident on the problem page. Although the problems are personal, and therefore seek personal solutions, Winship argues that 'unless women have access to knowledge which explains personal lives in social terms ... the onus on "you" to solve "your" problem is likely to be intimidating or ... only lead to frustrated "solutions" ' (80). Winship gives the example of a letter about a husband (with a sexual past) who cannot forget or forgive his wife's sexual past. As Winship points out, a personal solution to this problem cannot begin to tackle the social and cultural heritage of the sexual double standard. To pretend otherwise is to mislead.

> Agony aunties (and magazines) act as 'friends' to women – they bring women together in their pages – and yet by not

providing the knowledge to allow women to see the history of their common social condition, sadly and ironically, they come between women, expecting, and encouraging, them to do alone what they can only do together. (80)

READING VISUAL CULTURE

Magazines and newspapers consist of more than words on the page. Their popularity is unthinkable without taking into account the photographs, the illustrations and the advertisements which appear on almost every page. Undoubtedly the most influential work on popular visual culture within cultural studies is the foundational work of the French cultural theorist Roland Barthes.

Barthes's (1973) aim is to make explicit what too often remains implicit in the texts and practices of popular culture. His guiding principle is always interrogate 'the falsely obvious' (11). As he stated in the 'Preface' to the 1957 edition of *Mythologies* (one of the founding texts of cultural studies), 'I resented seeing Nature and History confused at every turn, and I wanted to track down, in the decorative display of *what-goes-without-saying*, the ideological abuse which, in my view, is hidden there' (11).

Barthes's early work on popular culture is concerned with the process of 'signification', the means by which meanings are produced and circulated. He uses Saussure's linguistic model (see chapter 4 above) to analyse the texts and practices of French popular culture. He takes Saussure's schema of signifier + signified = sign and adds to it a second level of signification. As noted in chapter 4, the signifier 'cat' produces the signified 'cat': a primary signification. The sign 'cat' produced in this formulation can become the signifier 'cat' in a second level of signification. This produces at the secondary level the signified 'cat': 'a woman who gossips maliciously' (*Collins English Dictionary*). As the diagram illustrates (Figure 3), the sign of primary signification becomes the signifier of secondary signification. In *Elements of Semiology* (1967), Barthes substitutes the more familiar terms 'denotation' (primary signification) and 'connotation' (secondary signification).

87

Primary signification Denotation	1. Signifier	2. Signified	
Secondary signification Connotation	3. Sign I. SIGNIFIER		II. SIGNIFIED
	III. SIGN		

Figure 3

Barthes (1973) claims that it is at the level of secondary signification or connotation that what he calls 'myth' is produced and made
available for consumption. By myth, Barthes means ideology understood as a body of ideas and practices which defend and actively promote the values and interests of the dominant groups in society. Perhaps Barthes's most famous example of the workings of secondary
signification is taken from the cover of *Paris Match* (1955). Here is
Barthes's account of his encounter with the cover of the magazine:

> I am at the barber's, and a copy of *Paris Match* is offered to me.
> On the cover, a young Negro in a French uniform is saluting,
> with his eyes uplifted, probably fixed on the fold of the tricol-
> our. All this is the meaning of the picture. But, whether naively
> or not, I see very well what is signifies to me: that France is a
> great Empire, that all her sons, without colour discrimination,
> faithfully serve under her flag, and that there is no better answer
> to the detractors of an alleged colonialism than the zeal shown
> by this Negro in serving his so-called oppressors. I am therefore
> faced with a greater semiological system: there is a signifier,
> itself already formed with a previous system (*a black soldier is
> giving the French salute*); there is a signified (it is a purposeful
> mixture of Frenchness and militariness); finally there is a
> presence of the signified through the signifier. (125–6)

At the level of primary signification (denotation), this is an image of a black soldier saluting the French flag, while at the level of secondary signification (connotation) it becomes *Paris Match*'s attempt to produce a positive image of French imperialism.

In 'The Photographic Message' (in *Image – Music – Text*, 1977), Barthes introduces a number of further considerations. Context of publication is important. If, for example, the photograph of the black soldier saluting the flag had appeared on the cover of a socialist magazine, its connotative meaning(s) would have been very different. Readers would have looked for irony. Rather than being read as a positive image of French imperialism, it would have been seen as a sign of imperial exploitation and manipulation. In addition to this, a socialist, for example, reading Barthes's copy of *Paris Match* would not have seen the image as a positive image of French imperialism, but as a desperate attempt to project such an image given the general historical context of France's defeat in Vietnam (1946–54) and its pending defeat in Algeria (1954–62). Despite all this, Barthes is clear about the intention behind the image:

> [m]yth has an imperative, buttonholing character ... [it arrests] in both the physical and the legal sense of the term: French imperialism condemns the saluting Negro to be nothing more than an instrumental signifier, the Negro suddenly hails me in the name of French imperialism; but at the same moment the Negro's salute thickens, becomes vitrified, freezes into an eternal reference meant to *establish* French imperialism. (1973: 134–5)

Barthes envisages three possible reading positions from which the image can be read. The first would simply see the black soldier saluting the flag as an 'example' of French imperialism, a 'symbol' for it. This is the position of those who produce such myths. The second would see the image as an 'alibi' of French imperialism. This would be the position of the socialist reader to whom Barthes might pass his copy of *Paris Match*. The final reading position is that of the 'reader of myths'. He or she reads the image not as an 'example' or a 'symbol', nor as an 'alibi'; quite simply, the black soldier saluting the flag 'is the very *presence* of French imperialism'. There is of course a fourth reading position, that of Barthes himself, the mythologist (producing what Barthes calls a 'structural description'). Barthes' is a reading position which seeks to determine the image's means of ideological production, its transformation of 'history' into 'nature' – the way in which the black soldier saluting the flag is made to seem to *naturally* conjure up the concept of French imperialism, to produce a situation in which there is nothing to discuss, it is so *obvious* that one implies the presence of the other. In this way, the relationship between the black soldier saluting the flag and French imperialism has been 'naturalized'. According to Barthes,

> what allows the reader to consume myth innocently is that he [sic] does not see it as a semiological system but as an inductive one. Where there is only equivalence, he sees a kind of causal process: the signifier and the signified have, in his eyes, a natural relationship. This confusion can be expressed otherwise: any semiological system is a system of values; now the myth-consumer takes the signification for a system of facts: myth is read as a factual system, whereas it is but a semiological system. (142)

Again, according to Barthes, '[s]emiology has taught us that myth has the task of giving a historical intention a natural justification, and making contingency appear eternal . . . myth is constituted by the loss of the historical quality of things: in it, things lose the memory that they once were made' (155). What is made to disappear from the image of the black soldier saluting the flag

> is the contingent, historical, in one word *fabricated* quality of colonialism. Myth does not deny things, on the contrary, its function is to talk about them; simply, it purifies them, it makes them innocent, it gives them a natural and eternal justification, it gives them a clarity which is not that of an explanation but that of a statement of fact. If I *state the fact* of French imperiality without explaining it, I am very near to finding that it is natural and *goes without saying*. . . . In passing from history to nature, myth acts economically: it abolished the complexity of human acts . . . it orgranizes a world which is without contradictions because it is without

depth, a world wide open and wallowing in the evident, it establishes a blissful clarity: things appear to mean something by themselves. (156)

Images rarely appear without the accompaniment of a linguistic text of one kind or another. A newspaper photograph, for example, will be surrounded by a title, a caption, a story and the general layout of the page. It will also, as we have already noted, be situated within the context of a particular newspaper or magazine. The context provided by the *Daily Mail* is very different from that provided by the *Socialist Worker*. Readership and reader expectation form part of this context. Barthes contends that 'the texts loads the image, burdening it with culture, a moral, an imagination' (1977: 26). The image does not illustrate the text; it is the text which amplifies the connotative potential of the image. Barthes refers to this process as 'relay'. The relationship can of course work in other ways. For example, rather than 'amplifying a set of connotations already given in the photograph . . . the text produces (invents) an entirely new signified which is retroactively projected into the image, so much so as to appear denoted there' (27). For example, a publicity photograph of a Hollywood actor, taken in 1994 to promote his latest film in which he plays a man who loses a fortune gambling, could be reused to accompany a newspaper report about the death of a close friend. The photograph is retitled: 'Cocaine killed my friend.' The caption would bleed into the image, producing (inventing) connotations of loss, despair, and a certain thoughtfulness about the role of drugs in Hollywood. Barthes refers to this process as 'anchorage'. What the example of the different meanings of the photograph of the film star reveal is the polysemic nature of all signs – that is, their potential for multiple signification. Without the addition of a linguistic text, the meaning of the image is very difficult to pin down. The linguistic message works in two ways. It helps the reader to identify the denotative meaning of the image: this is a film star looking reflective. Second, it limits the potential proliferation of the connotations of the image: the film star is reflective because of the drug overdose of one of his closest friends. Therefore, the film star is contemplating the role of drugs in Hollywood. Moreover, it tries to make the reader believe that the connotative meaning is actually present at the level of denotation.

What makes the move from denotation to connotation possible is the store of social knowledge (a cultural repertoire) upon which the reader is able to draw when he or she reads the image. Without access to this shared code (conscious or unconscious), the operations of connotations would not be possible. And of course such knowledge is always both historical and cultural. That is to say, it might differ from one culture to another, and from one period to another. Cultural difference might also be marked by differences of class, race and gender. However, as Barthes points out, '[t]he variation in readings is not, however, anarchic; it depends on the different kinds of knowledge – practical, national, cultural, aesthetic – invested in the image [by the reader]' (46). Here we see once again the analogy with language. The individual image is an example of 'parole', and the code of connotations is an example of 'langue' (see chapter 4 above). What makes meaning-production possible are the shared cultural codes upon which both the producers and consumers of an image are able to draw. Connotations are therefore not simply produced by the makers of the image, but are activated from an already existing and shared cultural repertoire. An image both draws from the cultural repertoire and at the same time adds to it. Moreover, the cultural repertoire does not form a homogenous block. Myth is continually confronted by counter-myth. For example, an image containing references to pop-music culture might be seen by a young audience as an index of freedom and heterogeneity, while to an older audience it might signal manipulation and homogeneity. Which codes are mobilised will largely depend on the triple context of the location of the text, the historical moment and the cultural formation of the reader.

6

POPULAR MUSIC

Popular music is everywhere. It has become more and more an unavoidable part of our lives. In my youth I had to seek it out. Now it seems to appear everywhere I go. We encounter it in the shopping mall, the supermarket, on the streets, at work, in parks, in pubs, in clubs, in restaurants and cafes, on the television, at the cinema, on the radio. In addition, we can locate it in music stores, in our individual music collections, on jukeboxes, at concerts and festivals. Our musical choices contribute to our sense of self. They also contribute to the economic well-being of the music industry. In recent times, popular music's undoubted cultural and economic significance has brought it more centrally into the focus of cultural studies.

THE POLITICAL ECONOMY OF POPULAR MUSIC

According to Simon Frith (1983), the work of Theodor Adorno, a leading member of the Frankfurt School, represents 'the most systematic and the most searing analysis of mass culture and the most challenging for anyone claiming even a scrap of value for the products that come churning out of the music industry' (44). In 1941, Adorno published a very influential essay called 'On Popular Music' (in Storey 1994). In the essay, he makes three specific claims about popular music. First, he claims that it is 'standardized'. 'Standardization', as Adorno points out, 'extends from the most general features to the most specific ones' (202–3). Once a musical and/or lyrical pattern has proved successful, it is exploited to commercial exhaustion, culminating in 'the crystallization of standards' (204). Moreover, details from one popular song can be interchanged with details from another. Unlike the organic structure of 'serious music' (Beethoven, for example), where each detail expresses the whole, popular music is mechanical in the sense that a given detail can be shifted from one song to another without any real effect on the structure as a whole. In order to conceal standardisation, the music industry engages in what Adorno calls 'pseudo-individualization': '[s]tandardization of song hits keeps the customers in line by doing their listening for them, as it were. Pseudo-individualization, for its part, keeps them in line by making them forget that what they listen to is already listened to for them, or "pre-digested" ' (206).

Adorno's second claim is that popular music promotes passive listening. Work under capitalism is dull and therefore promotes the search for escape, but, because it is also dulling, it leaves little energy for real escape – the demands of 'authentic' culture; instead, refuge is sought in forms such as popular music. The consumption of popular music is always passive, and endlessly repetitive, confirming the world as it is. 'Serious' music plays to the pleasure of the imagination, offering an engagement with the world as it could be. Popular music is the 'non-productive correlate' to life in the office or on the factory floor. The 'strain and boredom' of work leads men and women to the 'avoidance of effort' in their leisure time. Denied 'novelty' in their work time, and too exhausted for it in their leisure time, 'they crave a stimulant': popular music satisfies the craving.

> Its stimulations are met with the inability to vest effort in the ever-identical. This means boredom again. It is a circle which makes escape impossible. The impossibility of escape causes the widespread attitude of inattention toward popular music. The moment of recognition is that of effortless sensation. The sudden attention attached to this moment burns itself out

instanter and relegates the listener to a realm of inattention and distraction. (211)

Popular music operates in a kind of tired dialectic: to consume it demands inattention and distraction, while its consumption produces in the consumer inattention and distraction.

Adorno's third point is the claim that popular music operates as 'social cement' (211). Its 'socio-psychological function' is to achieve in the consumers of popular music 'psychical adjustment to the mechanisms of present-day life' (211–12). This 'adjustment' manifests itself in 'two major socio-psychological types of mass behaviour . . . the "rhythmically" obedient type and the "emotional" type' (212). The first dances in distraction to the rhythm of his or her own exploitation and oppression. The second wallows in sentimental misery, oblivious to the real conditions of existence.

The political economy of culture has much in common with Adorno's approach. According to Peter Golding and Graham Murdock (1991), two distinguished exponents of the approach, political economy of culture

> focus[es] on the interplay between the symbolic and economic dimensions of public communications [including popular music]. It sets out to show how different ways of financing and organizing cultural production have traceable consequences for the range of discourses and representations in the public domain and for audiences' *access* to them (my italics). (15)

The significant word here is 'access' (privileged over 'use' and 'meaning'). This reveals the limitations of the approach: good on the economic dimensions but weak on the symbolic. Too often, political economy's idea of cultural analysis seems to involve little more than detailing access to, and availability of, cultural texts and practices. Political economy rarely advocates a consideration of what these texts and practices might actually mean (textually) or be made to mean in actual use (consumption). As Golding and Murdock point out, 'in contrast to recent work on audience activity within cultural studies, which concentrates on the negotiation of textual interpretations and media use in immediate social settings, critical

95

political economy seeks to relate variations in people's responses to their overall location in the economic system' (27). This seems to suggest that audience negotiations are fictitious, merely illusory moves in a game of economic power. While it is clearly important to locate the texts and practices of, say, popular music within the field of their economic determinations, it is clearly insufficient to do this and think you have also analysed important questions of audience appropriation and use. Political economy threatens, despite its admirable intentions, to collapse everything back into the economic.[1]

The political economy of culture approach fixes its gaze almost exclusively on the power of the music industry. Leon Rosselson's (1979) argument is typical:

> More than any of the other performing arts, the world of song is dominated by the money men on the one hand and the moral censors of the media on the other. The possibility of alternative voices making themselves heard is always small and at times, such as now [1979], non-existent. The illusion is that song is a freely available commodity. . . . The reality is that song is the private property of business organisations. (40–1)

The assumption being made is that the music industry determines the use value of the products which it produces. At best, the audiences passively consume what is offered by the music industry; at worse, they are cultural dupes, ideologically manipulated by the music which they consume. Rosselson, for example, claims that the music industry gives 'the public what they want it to want' (42). The claim is that how something is produced determines how it can be consumed. The music industry is a capitalist industry, therefore its products are capitalist products and, as such, bearers of capitalist ideology.

Rosselson contends that 'folk music' (both because of its origins in pre-capitalist societies and its 'anti-commercial' practices under capitalism) is an alternative music to the capitalist music of the music industry. Pop music 'is incapable of saying anything valuable about the world in which most people live, love and work' (47). 'Folk music' is offered as a genuine music of 'the people'. How does he know? He knows because of a competition run by the *Sunday Times*:

> when the *Sunday Times* ran a competition for the best song written about a sporting hero, not one of the thousand entries received used a rock idiom or even in the more middle-of-the-road pop ballad. Three-quarters of them used what could loosely be described as a folk or broadside ballad idiom. . . . Clearly, when people have a need to express themselves on any subject other than teenage love, they find no useful model in the rock or pop idiom. The folk tradition . . . is still found to be serviceable. (50)

One might of course wonder whether the readership of the *Sunday Times* and the audience at folk clubs (no doubt there is considerable overlap between the two) provide a fully adequate definition of 'the people'.

There can be no doubt that the music industry has enormous economic and cultural power. But does it follow from this that consumers are totally powerless? As Simon Frith (1983) points out, 'about 10 per cent of all records released (a little less for singles, a little more for LPs) make money' (147). Rather than dictating to a passive market, the music industry finds it very difficult to control the musical tastes of consumers. This is because there is always a difference between exchange value ('economic' value) and use value ('cultural' value). The music industry can control the first, but it is consumers who *make* the second.

Those on the moral and pessimistic left who attack the capitalist relations of consumption miss the point: it is the capitalist relations of production that justify its overthrow and not the consumer choice enabled by the capitalist market. Moral leftists and left pessimists have allowed themselves to become trapped in an elitist and reactionary argument which claims that more (quantity) always means less (quality). Moreover, as Terry Lovell (1983) indicates, the commodities from which popular culture (including popular music) is made

> have different use-values for the individuals who use and purchase them than they have for the capitalists who produce

and sell them, and in turn, for capital*ism* as a whole. We may assume that people do not purchase these cultural artefacts *in order* to expose themselves to bourgeois ideology . . . but to satisfy a variety of different wants which can only be guessed at in the absence of analysis and investigation. There is no guarantee that the use-value of the cultural object for its purchaser will even be compatible with its utility to capitalism as bourgeois ideology. (60)

It is important to distinguish between the power of the culture industries and the power of their influence. Too often the two are conflated, but they are not necessarily the same. The trouble with the political economy of culture approach is that it is usually assumed that they are the same. EMI is undoubtedly a powerful multinational capitalist record company, dealing in capitalist commodities. But once this is established, what next? Does it follow, for example, that EMI's products are the bearers of capitalist ideology? Those who buy EMI's records, or pay to see EMI performers play live, are in effect really buying capitalist ideology; being duped by a capitalist record company; being reproduced as capitalist subjects, ready to spend more and more money and consume more and more ideology? The problem with this approach is that it fails to fully acknowledge that capitalism produces commodities on the basis of their exchange value, whereas people tend to consume the commodities of capitalism on the basis of their use value. Commodities are valued for their symbolic significance. Consumption is an active, creative and productive process, concerned with pleasure, identity and the production of meaning. There are in effect two economies running in parallel courses: the economy of use and the economy of exchange. We do not understand one by only interrogating the other.

The situation is further complicated by tensions between particular capitals and capitalism as a whole. Common class interest – unless specific restraints, censorship etc. are imposed – usually take second place to the interests of particular capitals in search of surplus value.

> If surplus value can be extracted from the production
> of cultural commodities which challenge, or even subvert,

the dominant ideology, then all other things being equal it is in the interests of particular capitals to invest in the production of such commodities. Unless collective class restraints are exercised, the individual capitalists' pursuit of surplus value may lead to forms of cultural production which are against the interests of capitalism as a whole. (Lovell 1983: 61)

To explore this possibility would require specific focus on consumption as opposed to production. This is not to deny the claim of political economy of culture approach that a full analysis must take into account technological and economic determinations. But it is to insist that if our focus is consumption then our focus must be consumption as it is experienced and not as it should be experienced given the relations of production.

Far from creating and manipulating a passive audience, the various parts of the music industry live or die by their ability to respond to *active* consumption. As Frith (1983) points out, the music industry 'doesn't sell some single, hegemonic idea, but is, rather, a medium through which hundreds of competing ideas flow' (270). Attempts may be made to give some commercial shape to these ideas; but ultimately, as Frith indicates, 'efficient profit-making involves not the creation of "new needs" and audience "manipulation" but, rather, the response to existing needs and audience "satisfaction" ' (270). The music industry may control and determine the repertoire (what music is produced), but it cannot control and determine how the music is used and, moreover, the meaning(s) which it is given by those who use it.

YOUTH AND POP MUSIC

The cultural studies study of pop-music culture begins proper with the work of Stuart Hall and Paddy Whannel (1964). As they point out, '[t]he picture of young people as innocents exploited' by the pop-music industry 'is over-simplified' (269). Against this, they argue that there is very often conflict between the use made of a text or practice by an audience, and the use intended by the producers. Significantly, they concede that although '[t]his conflict is particularly marked in the field of teenage entertainment . . . it is to some extent common to the whole area of mass entertainment in a commercial setting' (270). Pop-music culture – songs, magazines, concerts, festivals, comics, interviews with pop stars, films, etc. – helps to establish a sense of identity among youth:

> [t]he culture provided by the commercial entertainment market . . . plays a crucial role. It mirrors attitudes and sentiments which are already there, and at the same time provides an expressive field and a set of symbols through which these attitudes can be projected. . . . Teenage culture is a contradictory mixture of the authentic and manufactured: it is an area of self-expression for the young and a lush grazing pasture for the commercial providers. (276)

Moreover, pop songs

> reflect adolescent difficulties in dealing with a tangle of emotional and sexual problems. They invoke the need to experience life directly and intensely. They express the drive for security in an uncertain and changeable emotional world. The fact that they are produced for a commercial market means that the songs and settings lack a certain authenticity. Yet they dramatize authentic feelings. They express vividly the adolescent emotional dilemma. (280)

Pop music exhibits 'emotional realism'; young men and women 'identify with these collective representations and . . . use them as guiding fictions. Such symbolic fictions are the folklore by means of which the teenager, in part, shapes and composes his mental picture of the world' (281). Hall and Whannel also identify the way in which teenagers use particular ways of talking, particular places to go, particular ways of dancing, and particular ways of dressing, to establish distance from the world of adults: they describe dress style as 'a minor popular art . . . used to express certain contemporary attitudes . . . for example, a strong current of social nonconformity and rebelliousness' (282). This line of investigation would come to full fruition in the work of the Centre for Contemporary Cultural Studies in the 1970s, under the directorship of Hall himself. But here, Hall and Whannel draw back from the full possibilities of their inquiries, anxious that an 'anthropological . . . slack relativism', with its focus on the functionality of pop-music culture, would prevent them from posing questions of value and quality, about likes ('are those likes enough?') and needs ('are the needs healthy ones?') and taste ('perhaps tastes can be extended').

Hall and Whannel compare pop music unfavourably with jazz. They claim that jazz is 'infinitely richer . . . both aesthetically and emotionally' (311). They also claim that the comparison is 'much more rewarding' than the more usual comparison between pop music and classical music, as both jazz and pop are popular musics. In the case of classical against pop, the comparison is always to show the banality of pop and to say something about those who consume it. Is Hall and Whannel's comparison fundamentally any different?

> The point behind such comparisons sought not to be *simply* to wean teenagers away from the juke-box heroes, but to alert them to the severe limitations and ephemeral quality of music which is so formula-dominated and so directly attuned to the standards set by the commercial market. It is a genuine widening of sensibility and emotional range which we should be working for – an extension of tastes which might lead to an extension of pleasure. The worst thing which we would say of pop music is not that it is vulgar, or morally wicked, but, more simply, that much of it is not very good. (311–12)

SUBCULTURES, ETHNOGRAPHY AND STRUCTURAL HOMOLOGIES

It is through rituals of consumption that subcultures form meaningful identities (see chapter 7 below). The selective appropriation and group use of what the market makes available work together to define, express, reflect and resonate group distinction and difference. The classic statement of this process is made by Hall and Jefferson in *Resistance through Rituals* (1976): 'This involves members of a group in the appropriation of particular objects which are, or can be made, "homologous" with their focal concerns, activities, group structure and collective self-image – objects in which they see their central values held and reflected' (56).

One such object is music. Subcultural use of music is perhaps music consumption at its most active. The consumption of music is one of the means through which a subculture forges its identity and culturally reproduces itself by marking its distinction and difference from other members of society. This is not a refusal to recognise the economic and cultural power of the music industry, but an insistence that pop music (like all commercially-provided popular culture) is a contradictory terrain. As Iain Chambers (1985) contends,

> For after the commercial power of the record companies has been recognised, after the persuasive sirens of the radio acknowledged, after the recommendations of the music press noted, it is finally those who buy the records, dance to the rhythms and live to the beat who demonstrate, despite the determined conditions of its production, the wider potential of pop. (xii)

Subcultural use of music was first noted by the American sociologist David Riesman (1990). Writing in 1950, he noted how the audience for popular music could be divided into two groups, 'a majority one, which accepts the adult picture of youth somewhat uncritically, and a minority one in which certain socially rebellious themes are encapsulated' (8). As he pointed out, the minority group is always small. Its rebellion takes a symbolic form:

> an insistence on rigorous standards of judgement and taste . . . a preference for the uncommercialized, unadvertised small bands rather than name bands; the development of a private language and then a flight from it when the private language (the same is true of other aspects of private style) is taken over by the majority group. (9–10)

Thus, consuming a particular music becomes a *way of being* in the world. Music consumption is used as a sign by which the *young* judge and are judged by others. To be part of a youth subculture is to display one's musical taste and to claim that its consumption is an act of communal creation. It does not matter, according to Riesman, whether the community is real or imagined. What is important is that the music provides a *sense* of community. It is a community created

102

in the act of consumption: '[w]hen he [sic] listens to music, even if no one else is around, he listens in a context of imaginary "others" – his listening is indeed often an effort to establish connection with them' (10).

In *Profane Culture* (1978), Paul Willis argues that the 'best ethnography does something which theory and commentary cannot: it presents human experience without minimizing it, and without making it a passive reflex of social structure and social conditions' (170). Ethnography allows the cultural worker to reproduce what Willis calls 'the profane creativity of living cultures' (170). The central concern of *Profane Culture* is the making of culture by 'oppressed, subordinate or minority groups'. Against the common view that such groups are manipulated by the culture industries, he insists that they 'can have a hand in the construction of their own vibrant cultures and are not merely cultural dupes: the fall guys in a social system stacked overwhelmingly against them and dominated by capitalist media and commercial provision' (1). People make culture through the transformation (what I described in chapter 1 above as 'production in use') of the texts and practices of the culture industries.

As part of his general investigation, Willis studies the music use of two subcultural groups, motorbike boys and hippies. His concern was to explore the 'homologies' between musical selection and taste and other aspects of group lifestyle. Homological analysis is essentially concerned with uncovering the extent to which particular texts and practices 'in their structure and content . . . parallel and reflect the structure, style, typical concerns, attitudes and feelings of the social group' (191). The purpose of homological analysis is to tease out the relationship between the particular cultural choices of a social group and how these are used to construct the cultural meaning of the social group.

Willis found that pop music was an integral part of the culture of the motorbike boys. The music of choice was the classic rock' n' roll of the late 1950s (perceived by the bike boys as a 'golden age' of pop music). Their musical preference ('deliberate choice', not 'passive reception') had 'the dialectical capacity . . . to reflect, resonate and return something of real value to the motor-bike boys'

(62). What the music returned was a sense of 'security, authenticity and masculinity' (63). Willis identifies four homologies between the subculture and its consumption of music. First, the historical unity of the music allowed its consumption to mark difference and distinction from those who consumed contemporary pop music. This provided the group with a sense of authenticity. Second, the music, especially early Elvis Presley and Buddy Holly, was seen to validate aggressive masculinity in its celebration (mostly articulated through vocal delivery and the energy of the music, rather than in its lyrical content) of a tough and physical response to an uncertain and uncaring world. Thus the music was seen to have the capacity to make concrete and to authenticate the group's commitment to displays of aggressive masculinity. Third, classic rock' n' roll was perceived as a music of movement (a music with beat) for a lifestyle of movement. Rock' n' roll was seen to articulate the bike boys' sense of a life of endless physical movement. They valued its 'fastness and clarity of beat' (68). Dancing and fast bike-riding are at the heart of this relationship. The pounding rhythm of the music could both incite and supply an imaginary soundtrack to the fast bike-riding of the motorbike boys. Being fast on the road was both a consequence of the music's meaning and a living out of that meaning. Fourth, the motorbike boys preferred singles to albums. The fact a song was not available as a single amounted to a declaration of its worthlessness. For a culture which valued concrete experience over mental activity, listening to albums implied a level of seriousness and musical indulgence foreign to the motorbike boys. Singles put the listener in control; albums implied a commitment beyond the realm of the concrete now.

Willis's investigations of hippy culture revealed the mediating role which drugs, especially acid (LSD: lysergic acid diethylamide) and cannabis played in the consumption of music. It was a common belief that drug use enhanced the appreciation and understanding of music. This view was compounded by the belief (not unfounded) that the principal musicians of the counterculture had themselves experimented with drugs. Drug use was thus seen as a connection between audience and performers: it was the central articulating principle of the hippy culture. It was a culture expressed through the production and consumption of a particular type of music made and consumed in the context of a particular type of drug use. But the coming together (the dialectical interplay) of experiments with hallucinogenics and experiments with making music led to an esoteric (and often elitist) celebration of the very 'meaninglessness' of the music (a refusal to meaning and meaningfulness). It was this which kept the 'secret' at the heart of the hippy culture. 'Straights' were excluded because they lacked access to the 'secret' code, only available through the experience of the dialectical interplay of drugs and music.

Willis discovered that, like the motorbike boys, the hippies were deliberate in their choice of music. The music of preference was so-called 'progressive' rock. Unlike the bike boys, the hippies did not use music as an imaginary soundtrack to fast riding or as a means to engage the body in dance. For the hippies, music was not a means to something else, it was an 'experience' in its own right. Music was for 'concentrated listening'. The hippies interviewed by Willis preferred the relatively uninterrupted flow of an album to the episodic burst of the three-minute single.

A major difference between the two cultures is that whereas the motorbike boys made their culture from a musical repertoire made available to them by the culture industries and had no influence on and interaction with the repertoire from which they made their culture. Hippy culture produced the musicians who in turn produced hippy culture. Many of Willis's interviewees knew famous musicians and expected to come into contact with others. As one of his interviewees told him, 'The bands that are producing music today are coming out of this life-style, they are only projecting what we are thinking. They are coming from this life-style, they are growing from us, and they are communicating what we already know' (165).

Willis sees the achievements of both groups in having demonstrated the 'profane' power of subordinate and marginal groups 'to sometimes take as their own, select and creatively develop particular artefacts to express their own meanings' (166).

WORDS AND MUSIC: MAKING PLAIN TALK DANCE

When we say popular music, we mostly have in mind songs. And if we ask the question 'what does this song mean?' too often we respond by referring to the content of the lyrics. But the meaning of a song cannot be reduced to the words on the page. As Griel Marcus puts it, 'words are sounds we can feel before they are statements to understand' (quoted in Frith 1983: 14). Lyrics are written to be performed. They only really come to life in the performance of a singer.

> In songs, words are the signs of a voice. A song is always a performance and song words are always spoken out – vehicles for the voice . . . structures of sound that are *direct* signs of emotion and marks of character . . . Pop songs celebrate not the articulate but the inarticulate, and the evaluation of pop singers depends not on words but on sounds – on the noises around the words. (Frith 1983: 35)

The noises around the words – the inability, for example, to find the right words and therefore to make do with everyday language – is the sign of real emotion and sincerity. 'Inarticulateness, not poetry, is the popular songwriter's conventional sign of sincerity' (Frith 1983: 35).

The celebration of the inarticulate takes many forms. Frith gives the example of soul music: 'the best of soul conviction is the singer's way with non-words' (36). Think of, for example, Otis Redding's struggle to enunciate the right words to express the pain of possible loss in 'I've Been Loving You Too Long' (1965). An analysis based on the song lyrics alone would not be able to capture the emotional force of Redding's performance.

This recalls what Roland Barthes (1977) calls the 'grain' of the voice, 'the body in the voice as it sings' (118). He writes of an escape from the 'tyranny of meaning'. The pleasure of music is not the pleasure of the representation of something that has happened elsewhere (a reflection of meaning) but the pleasure of what is being made (the making and materiality of meaning). The pleasure and power of popular music is not in the performance of emotion but in the emotion of performance. Barthes's argument is part of a general argument about the difference between 'plaisir' and 'jouissance'. Plaisir refers to 'a pleasure . . . linked to cultural enjoyment and identity' (1975: 9). It is the pleasure of convention and recognition. Jouissance, on the other hand, refers to orgasmic moments of release, beyond meaning. Richard Middleton (1990) gives the example of the difference(s) between Elvis Presley and his contemporary Pat Boone.

> Presley's singing . . . *disrupts* language through a vivid staging of the vocal body, while Boone, marketed as a 'safe' alternative, offers unequivocal meaning in which words, melody and tone fuse into a predictable structure. . . . Notice that this is not the same explanation as the usual one – that Boone 'cleaned up' Presley by exorcizing sex; there seems little doubt that Boone's fans heard him as 'sexy'. The difference lies rather in the *way* 'sex' is channelled. To an unusual degree, Presley offered an individual body, unique, untranslatable, outside the familiar cultural framework, exciting and dangerous; in Boone we hear a generalized image, the energy *bound*, tied into the conventional thoughts and sentiments provoked by the words and the intonational rhetoric – safe because explicit and unambiguous. (263)

What Middleton is arguing (following Barthes) is that Presley's performance, unlike that of Boone, goes beyond a performance of the song's meaning. Or, to put it another way, the meaning of a Presley performance is in the performance itself: 'the body in the voice as it sings' producing significance beyond the 'tyranny of meaning'. Presley's performance is not an invitation to meaning and understanding but an invitation to be lost in music, to be overwhelmed by jouissance.

In many ways, this is a distinction between 'performance' and 'message'. It helps explain how one can enjoy songs with politics which one would reject in another context. For example, Simon Frith and Angela McRobbie (1978) derive pleasure from Tammy Wynette's 'Stand By Your Man' despite rejecting its apparent articulation of patriarchal ideology (4). On a personal note,

Barthes's notion of the 'grain' of the voice helped me to understand my own pleasure in Bob Dylan's vocal delivery (especially on the albums recorded in the mid-1960s). I had always (more or less) thought, until reading Barthes, that my pleasure derived from the lyrical eloquence of the songs. Yet I could never understand why so many covers of his material left me cold. Barthes's notion of the 'grain' seems to offer a solution to the real source of my pleasure.

But denying the significance of meaning in a rush to celebrate jouissance has its own problems. There is a danger here of celebrating pleasure and ignoring politics (see the next section below). Moreover, to acknowledge that a song's significance cannot be reduced to its lyrical content should not lead to a dismissal of the importance of the words altogether.

> Pop lyricists work on the ordinariness of langauge. They make our most commonplace words and phrases suddenly seem full of sly jokes and references. With an array of verbal bricks and playful clichés, good lyricists, from Bob Dylan to Ira Gershwin, add to our sense of *common* language. Their songs are about words: they give us new ways to mouth the commonplaces of daily discourse. (Frith 1983: 37)

In other words, pop songs have

> the power to make ordinary language intense and vital; the words then resonate – they bring a touch of fantasy into our mundane use of them. Pop songs work precisely insofar as they are *not* poems. . . . The pop song banalities people pick up on are, in general, not illuminating but encouraging: they give emotional currency to the common phrases that are all most people have for expressing their daily cares. The language that hems us in suddenly seems open – if we can't speak in poetry, we can speak in pop songs. They give us a way to *refuse* the mundane. (38)

Criticisms of the supposed banality of the lyrics of pop music, therefore, miss the point. The words of pop music are not intended to be poetry (and attempts to claim them as such are misguided). Pop music takes the language of the everyday – the cliché, the trite remark, the commonplace – and stages them in an affective play of voice and performance. Again, to quote Frith (1983), the result is 'to make plain talk dance ... to make ordinary language intense and vital; the words then resonate – they bring a touch of fantasy into our mundane use of them' (37–8).

POLITICS AND POP MUSIC[2]

Politics enters a different moments in the making of pop music: production, distribution, performance, consumption, etc. At the level of 'common sense', political pop is simply pop that is *political* – pop music which contains an overtly political commentary on the world. In this section, I will attempt to problematise this contention.

Politics is about power, and pop music can be powerful. Politicians have long realised this. They have often dreamed of turning the taste communities of pop music into the voting constituencies of party politics. The prospect of the votes of the young has tempted many a politician into pop music. In 1965, Harold Wilson's courting of the Beatles resulted in their being awarded MBEs. As Robin Denselow (1989) explains, 'in his early campaigns he was only too pleased to be photographed puffing his pipe alongside these charming, cute and utterly safe-seeming mop-tops who were working such wonders for the British balance of payments' (92). Of course, the relationship soured somewhat in 1969, when John Lennon returned his award in protest at Britain's support for America's war in Vietnam. But while it lasted, it was political pop. There are many other illustrations of such relationships. Jimmy Carter tried to use Bob Dylan, both Ronald Reagan and Walter Mondale tried to use Bruce Springsteen, and Neil Kinnock appeared in a Tracy Ullman video. All are examples of political pop.

Politicians involve themselves in pop music in other ways – for example, the demand for censorship. In 1977, the year of the Royal Silver Jubilee, pressure was exerted to ban the Sex Pistols' 'God Save the Queen'. The song was banned and went straight to number one. In other countries, censorship is much more harshly implemented. In pre-democratic South Africa, all lyric sheets had to be submitted

109

for official scrutiny before a song could be recorded. These are both instances of political pop.

Pop can be political if the musicians say it is. Taste communities can become political constituencies. West Coast rock was ideologically premised on opposition to America's war in Vietnam. It addressed its audience as actual or potential members of an 'alternative' society. Part of the sense of belonging involved an attitude to the Vietnam War. The prevalence of this anti-war feeling was such that, in the context of the counterculture, all songs were in a sense against the war. The fact that Country Joe and the Fish sang songs against the war was enough to make all their songs seem implicitly against the war. Opposition to the war was the central articulating principle of the counterculture: music both expressed the values and aspirations of the counterculture, while at the same time it helped consolidate and reproduce the culture. This is another example of political pop.

Sometimes the situation is more complex. For example, on their 1985 American tour, U2 found they had to explain the politics of their song 'Sunday, Bloody Sunday'. In performance after performance, Bono attacked what he regards as the senseless politics of Irish Americans who constantly refer to 'the war back home' with enthusiasm and excitement. 'Sunday, Bloody Sunday', he explained, is not a song in celebration of the IRA. Yet, despite Bono's protests to the contrary, the audience seemed determined to claim it for the American version of the Irish Revolution – in other words, to claim it as political pop.

The music industry has its own definition of political pop music: political pop as sales category. Certain pop – rap, or the work of Billy Bragg, for example – is marketed as political. Since the mid 1960s, record companies have been comfortably making money out of politics. By 1968, the music of the counterculture had begun to be marketed under slogans such as 'The revolutionaries are on Columbia'; 'Psychedelia – the sound of the NOW generation' (MGM). This is incorporation on a grand scale. When it comes to individual songs, their attitude is often quite different. Selling the music of a subculture, or of a particular genre, or even the work of a particular performer, as political is fine, but selling the individual political song is something quite different. In the unpredictable and ever-changing world of pop-music culture, individual political songs (cut loose from a movement, a genre, a profitable performer) are something that record companies would rather not handle. The big transnational record companies universalise their interests and profits by dealing in universals. The politics of profit which try to dictate the terms of the international market consider the political pop song to be too specific to make money. From the perspective of the music industry, political pop, unless it can be catalogued in a particular way, is financially far too risky. At home, these risks are of offending, of seeming too opinionated, of crossing the line between entertainment and dull social comment. Abroad, the risks are that the audience will not connect with the ideas and experiences dealt with in the song. Political pop (as defined by the industry) is a financial risk.

Another definition of political pop music is pop music *organised* politically. In 1976, Eric Clapton voiced his support for Enoch Powell's version of racism. Outrage within pop quickly solidified into the anti-racist umbrella organisation, Rock Against Racism (RAR). RAR was a united pop collective which staged concerts and festivals. Together with the Anti-Nazi League, RAR was successful in curbing the growth of organised racism. Political pop in the 1980s (using this definition) began with the release of the 'No Nukes' film and triple album featuring the performances of members of Musicians United For Safe Energy. The Sun City Project, established in 1985, united pop musicians in opposition to apartheid in a declared refusal to play the Sun City entertainment complex in South Africa. The result was a single, a video and an album. Live Aid, perhaps the key political pop event of the 1980s, reached an audience in excess of two billion. It gave famine both money and publicity. The following year, Amnesty International's *Conspiracy of Hope* tour played for a week across America from San Francisco to New York. As a result, Amnesty International doubled its membership in the USA. Two years later, it organised the *Amnesty International World Tour*. Using pop music to establish constituencies for specific political campaigns makes pop music political. We can of course be cynical and suggest that some of the performers who have supported political campaigns have done so simply to sell records. Well-founded or not, such cynicism *should* not survive the witnessing of the deeply moving reception accorded to Nelson Mandela at Wembley in April 1990. However the performers were defining their presence that day, the audience clearly wanted to be part of a utopian-political moment when pop music mattered enough for the world's most famous political prisoner (released only two months earlier) to thank a pop-music audience because they 'chose to care'.

To call pop music political is to bring into play a diversity of meanings. Pop music can be political *simultaneously* in lots of different ways. As John Street (1986) puts it, '[t]he politics of music are a mixture of state policies, business practices, artistic choices and audience responses' (23). Each of these elements places restrictions on and offers possibilities for the politics of pop music.

NOTES

1. The political economy of culture approach puts most of its considerable critical energy into the moment of production. The moment of consumption is seen very much as a secondary moment. But as Karl Marx, from whom much of the authority of the approach derives, argues, 'consumption produces production . . . because a product . . . , unlike a mere natural object, proves itself to be, becomes a product only through consumption' (1973: 91).
2. This section is based on research carried out by myself and Debbie Johnson. For a full account, see Storey and Johnson (1994).

7

THE CONSUMPTION
OF EVERYDAY LIFE

Consumption emerges as a cultural concern in the late 1950s and early 1960s in debates about the development of 'consumer society'. It then becomes fully visible in cultural studies in the 1970s in work on how subcultures appropriate commodities to produce alternative and oppositional meanings. More recently, it can be found in studies of fan culture and in studies of shopping as popular culture. In this chapter, I will review some of the key features of this work.

THEORIES OF CONSUMPTION

The cultural analysis of consumption begins in the political concerns of Marxism. In order to understand the classical Marxist account of consumption, we must know something about how it conceives the difference between capitalist and pre-capitalist social formations. Pre-capitalist societies (feudalism in Britain, for example) were not consumer societies in that goods were made mostly for immediate consumption or use or to be exchanged for other goods. It is only after the collapse of feudalism and the emergence of capitalism, a system based on the market, on money and on profit, that consumption becomes detached from simple needs and emerges as a significant aspect of human activity.

For Karl Marx and Frederick Engels, the transition from feudalism to capitalism was a transition from production driven by need to production driven by profit. Moreover, in capitalist societies, workers make goods in return for wages. They do not own the goods; the goods are sold on the market at a profit. Therefore to get goods, workers have to buy them with money. Thus: workers become 'consumers', and we have the emergence of 'consumer society'. To ensure the making of profits, people must consume. Therefore, consumption is 'artificially' stimulated by advertising. One consequence of this is 'alienation'. According to Marx (1975; first published in 1844), alienation results from 'the fact that labour is external to the worker . . . the worker feels himself only when he is not working. . . . His labour is therefore . . . not the satisfaction of a need but a mere means to satisfy needs outside itself' (1975: 326).

In other words, men and women are denied identity in (uncreative) production, and are therefore forced to seek identity in (creative) consumption. But this is always little more than a hollow substitute (a 'fetish'). Moreover, the process is encouraged by the so-called ideology of consumerism – the suggestion that the meaning of our lives is to be found in what we consume, rather than in what we produce. Thus the ideology legitimates and encourages the profit-making concerns of capitalism (a system demanding an ever-increasing consumption of goods).

Herbert Marcuse (1968) develops this line of argument, to suggest that the ideology of consumerism generates false needs and that these needs work as a form of social control: 'The people recognize themselves in their commodities; they find their soul in their automobile, hi-fi set, split-level home, kitchen equipment. The very mechanism which ties the individual to his society has changed; and social control is anchored in the new needs which it has produced' (9). Thus, according to Marcuse, adverts generate false needs – for example, the desire to be a certain kind of person, wearing a particular type of clothes, eating a particular type of food, drinking particular drinks, using particular items, etc.

The poststructuralist psychoanalysis of Jacques Lacan also offers a model for thinking critically about consumption. The 'ideology of consumerism' works in much the same way as the 'ideology of romance' (see Storey 1993). The ideology of romance is a

114

narrative constructed around a quest: 'love' is the solution to all problems; 'love' makes us complete; 'love' makes us full; 'love' makes us whole. Like the search for 'love', consumption implies an incompleteness; something missing. And from the perspective of Lacanian psychoanalysis, in both ideologies what is missing is the same: the mother's body. According to Lacan (see chapter 4 above for a more detailed account), the move from the 'imaginary' to the 'symbolic' is a move from the 'full' world of the mother's body to the 'empty' world of language and 'selfhood'. Clearly, it is a transition experienced as loss. We were whole then, complete, before the construction of separate sense of 'self' (i.e. separate from the mother). The consequence is that we spend the rest of our lives trying to return to the fullness of the 'imaginary'. We engage in an endless quest to return, but make do instead with substitute objects, with displacement strategies. As Terry Eagleton (1983) explains, 'In Lacanian theory, it is an original lost object – the mother's body – which drives forward the narrative of our lives, impelling us to pursue substitutes for this lost paradise in the endless metonymic movement of desire' (185).

The 'ideology of consumerism' can be seen as one of these displacement strategies; one example of this endless search, the endless metonymic movement of desire. The promise which it makes is that (like 'love') consumption is the answer to all our problems; consumption will make us whole again; consumption will make us full again; consumption will make us complete again; consumption will return us to the blissful state of the 'imaginary'. This perhaps makes some sense of the appeal of a card that John Fiske (1989b) found while browsing in a gift shop in Australia. The inscription read: 'Work to Live, Live to Love, and Love to Shop, so you see . . . if I can buy enough things I'll never have to work at love again' (18).

Pierre Bourdieu (1984) shifts the argument from what consumption does to us to how we use consumption for purposes of social distinction. He contends that the culture of living (lifestyle, etc.) is a significant area of struggle between social groups and classes. For Bourdieu, the consumption of culture is 'predisposed, consciously and deliberately or not, to fulfil a social function of legitimating social differences' (5). For example, culture is use by the dominant class, according to Bourdieu, to ensure its reproduction as the dominant class. Bourdieu's purpose is not to state or prove the self-evident, that different classes have different lifestyles, different taste(s) in culture, etc., but to interrogate the processes by which the making of cultural distinctions secures and legitimates forms of power and domination which are ultimately rooted in economic inequality. In other words: he argues that although class rule is ultimately economic, the form which it takes is cultural; and that cultural distinction, the making, marking and maintaining of cultural difference, is the key to understanding this. Moreover, the dominant class's commitment to culture is an attempt to establish a mode of legitimation equivalent to the aristocracy's 'blood' or 'right of birth'. Thus: the source of difference is symbolically shifted from the economic field to the field of culture, making power appear to be the result of cultural distinction. In this way, the production and reproduction of cultural space produces and reproduces social space and class difference.

Using consumption to mark distinction and difference is not new. The American sociologist, Thorstein Veblen (1953), in *The Theory of the Leisure Class* (first published in 1899), identified a new bourgeois leisure class in America who used consumption to define themselves and their status. Instead of the more traditional means to articulate status – by work and occupation, etc., they articulated status through what Veblen called 'conspicuous consumption'. At more or less the same time, the German sociologist Georg Simmel (in Bocock and Thompson 1992), in an essay called 'The Metropolis and Mental Life' (1903), identified a similar mode of behaviour in the new distinctive urban culture of Berlin at the turn of the century. Confronted by the anonymity of city life, the new urban bourgeoisie used particular patterns of consumption to maintain and to display a sense of individuality. In order to deal with city life, individuals, according to Simmel, 'cultivate a sham individualism through the pursuit of signs of status, fashion, or marks of individual eccentricity' (126). Simmel argued that the 'significance' of such behaviour lies not in its particular content but 'in its form of being different, of making oneself stand out' (126). The class fractions identified by

Veblen and Simmel consumed to articulate a sense of identity and difference – to produce 'distinction'.

In the late 1950s and early 1960s – the moment of 'mass consumption' – the nature of consumption changes radically. During this period there is for the first time sufficient relative affluence for working people to consume on the basis of 'desire' rather than 'need': televisions, fridges, cars, vacuum cleaners, foreign holidays, etc. Moreover, this period marks the emergence of working people using patterns of consumption to articulate a sense of identity. I think it is significant that it is now that consumption emerges as a cultural concern in debates about the development of a so-called 'consumer society'. This is also the moment of the emergence of what is now called postmodernism. One aspect of postmodernism (and especially anxieties about postmodernism) may well be the proliferation 'downwards' of the use of consumption to articulate identity.

SUBCULTURAL CONSUMPTION

The cultural studies approach to youth subcultural consumption (see chapter 6 above for a review of the subcultural use of music) begins with Phil Cohen's (1972/1980) foundational analysis of working-class culture and youth subcultures in the East End of London. Cohen contends that youth subcultures are an attempt to solve problems experienced by the parent culture. From the mid-1950s onwards, the working class had been confronted by two contradictory discourses: the new ideology of affluence and 'conspicuous consumption' and the traditional claims of working-class life. Changes in local manufacturing (resulting in 'de-skilling') and changes in the local environment (high-rise flats) had together undermined traditional working-class life without increasing access to the new 'affluent society'.

> It seems to me that the latent function of subculture is this: to express and resolve, albeit 'magically', the contradictions which remain hidden or unresolved in the parent culture. The succession of subcultures which this parent culture generated

117

> can thus all be considered so many variations on a central theme – the contradiction, at an ideological level, between traditional working-class puritanism and the new hedonism of consumption; at an economic level, between a future as part of the socially mobile elite or as part of the new lumpen proletariat. Mods, parkas, skinheads, crombies all represent, in their different ways, an attempt to retrieve some of the socially cohesive elements destroyed in their parent culture and to combine these with elements selected from other class fractions, symbolizing one or other of the options confronting it. (Cohen 1980: 82–3)

In other words, in a symbolic response to the break-up of traditional working-class culture, a succession of youth subcultures attempted to hold together traditional notions of working-class community, while at the same time taking part (through acts of selective appropriation and consumption) in the opportunities presented by the 'affluent society'. For example, although mods tended to be employed in low-paid work, with few career opportunities, the style of the mod could be seen to represent 'an attempt to realise, but in an *imaginary relation* the conditions of existence of the socially mobile white collar worker'. Similarly, although they shared many of the traditional values of their parent culture ('their argot and ritual forms'), 'their dress and music reflected the hedonistic image of the affluent consumer' (Cohen 1980: 83). Thus subcultures represent 'a compromise solution to two contradictory needs: the need to create and express *autonomy* and *difference* from parents ... and the need to maintain ... *parental identifications*' (84). Or, as Dick Hebdige (1979) explains it,

> mods were negotiating changes and contradictions which were simultaneously affecting the parent culture but they were doing so in the terms of their own relatively autonomous problematic – by inventing an 'elsewhere' (the week-end, the West End) which was defined *against* the familiar locales of the home, the pub, the working-man's club, the neighbourhood. (79)

John Clarke et al. (1976) elaborate Cohen's approach by situating youth subcultures in terms of both the parent culture (the working-class culture of parents, non-subcultural peers, etc.) and the dominant culture. Following Cohen's lead, they approach youth subcultures as 'coded' representations of conflicts and contradictions affecting the working class as a whole. Using Antonio Gramsci's theory of hegemony, they argue that the struggles of youth subcultures could now be located in the wider class struggle. Hebdige (1979) shifts the emphasis from class politics to the politics of style. As he explains, 'the challenge to hegemony which subcultures represent is not issued directly by them. Rather it is expressed obliquely, in style' (17). For example, in an earlier discussion of subcultures, Hebdige (1976) claims of mod style:

> The style they created . . . constituted a parody of the consumer society in which they were situated. The mod dealt his [sic] blows by inverting and distorting the images (of neatness, of short hair) so cherished by his [sic] employers and parents, to create a style, which while being overtly close to the straight world was nonetheless incomprehensible to it. (93)

Youth subcultures communicate through acts of consumption. As Hebdige maintains, youth subcultures are 'concerned first and foremost with consumption' (Hebdige 1979: 94–5).

> They are . . . cultures of conspicuous consumption – even when, as with the skinheads and the punks, certain types of consumption are conspicuously refused – and it is through the distinctive rituals of consumption, through style, that the subculture at once reveals its 'secret' identity and communicates its forbidden meanings. It is basically the way in which commodities are *used* in subculture which mark the subculture off from more orthodox cultural formations. (102–3)

Subcultural consumption is consumption at its most discriminating. Through a process of 'bricolage', subcultures appropriate for

119

their own purposes and meanings the commodities commercially provided. Products are combined or transformed in ways not intended by their producers; commodities are rearticulated to produce oppositional meanings. Examples include Teddy Boys wearing Savile Row Edwardian jackets, mods wearing Italian suits, punks using bin-liners and safety pins. In this way (and through patterns of behaviour, ways of speaking, taste in music, etc.), youth subcultures engage in symbolic forms of resistance to both dominant and parent cultures. According to this model, youth subcultures always move from originality and opposition to commercial incorporation and ideological defusion as the culture industries eventually succeed in marketing subcultural resistance for general consumption and profit. As Hebdige explains, 'Youth cultural styles may begin by issuing symbolic challenges, but they must end by establishing new sets of conventions; by creating new commodities, new industries or rejuvenating old ones' (96).

Hebdige's approach represents an analytical move within cultural studies from the culturalism of Cohen (1980) and Clarke et al. (1976) to a methodology informed by the techniques of structuralism (see chapter 4 above; also Storey (1993) for a discussion of culturalism and structuralism in cultural studies). For Hebdige, style is not the *expression* of class location, it is a signifying system, communicating both cultural identity and cultural difference. Youth subcultures communicate their distinct identity and their difference from and in opposition to peer, parent and dominant cultures through a politics of style. The meaning of youth subcultures is always played out through style rather than as a struggle really taking place elsewhere.

Subcultural analysis has always tended to celebrate the extraordinary as against the ordinary. Subcultures represent youth in resistance, actively refusing to conform to the passive commercial tastes of the majority of youth. Once resistance has given way to incorporation, analysis stops, waiting for the next 'great refusal'. The move from subcultures to the consumption patterns of young people as a whole was developed around the recognition that all young people are active consumers of culture and not the passive cultural dupes of much subcultural theory. As Angela McRobbie (1994) explains,

> While the early days of subcultural theory from the Centre for Contemporary Cultural Studies (CCCS) it was important to draw a line between youth culture and pop culture, crediting the former with a form of symbolic class authenticity and the latter with all the marks of the consumer culture, in reality the two were always merged, involved in an ongoing relationship. (156)

This was part of a general move away from an 'elitist' view of youth culture organised around a binary opposition between resistant 'style' and conformist 'fashion', but it was also governed by an apparent breakdown of (or at the very least, a blurring of) the distinction between the two. According to McRobbie, the change 'reflected a situation in which youthfulness became virtually synonymous with subculture' (159) as subcultures proliferated and were recycled.

The approach to youth subcultures (from Cohen to Hebdige) has been challenged from *within* cultural studies on two counts. First, as Angela McRobbie and Jenny Garber (1976) asked, 'Are girls . . . *really* not active or present in youth subcultures? Or has something in the way this research is done rendered them invisible?' (209). The answer to the first question is that girls are active but often in different ways from boys. The answer to the second question was yes.

The introduction of gender has broadened the focus of cultural studies work on youth subcultures: for example, Angela McRobbie has introduced dance into cultural studies. Writing in 1984, she claims that 'when dance has found its way into accounts of working-class culture, it has tended to be either derided as trivial or else taken as a sign of moral degeneration' (1991: 132). She cites Richard Hoggart's *The Uses of Literacy* (first published in 1957), in which dancing is seen as just one part of a culture of femininity which is 'flighty, careless and inane' (Hoggart 1990: 51).

Dance is a form of artistic practice but it is also a social practice, a leisure activity, a ritual form of sexuality, a method of exercise and a means of communication, 'a way of speaking through the body' (McRobbie 1991: 195). According to McRobbie, 'Dance for girls

121

represents a public extension of the private culture of femininity which takes place outside the worried gaze of the moral guardians and indoors in the protected space of the home' (1991: 197). She is aware that dance can be a means of conforming to social expectations of femininity. Dance is seen as an appropriate means to instil in girls the 'feminine' attributes of grace and control. But she insists that

> dance carries enormously pleasurable qualities for girls and women which frequently seem to suggest a displaced, shared and nebulous eroticism rather than a straightforwardly romantic, heavily heterosexual 'goal-oriented' drive. As a purveyor of fantasy, dance has also addressed areas of absolute privacy and personal intimacy, especially important for women and girls. And there is I think a case which can be made for forms of fantasy, daydreaming, and 'abandon' to be interpreted as part of a strategy of resistance or opposition; that is, as marking out one of those areas which cannot be totally colonised. Dance and music play an important role in these small daily *evasions*, partly because they are so strongly inscribed, in our culture, within the realms of feeling and emotion. They are associated with being temporarily out of control, or out of the reaches of controlling forces. (1991: 134)

Moreover, dance offers 'the opportunity for fantasy' (144). Like the spectator in the darkness of the cinema, 'the dancer can retain some degree of anonymity or absorption . . . blotting-out of the self, a suspension of real, daylight consciousness, and an aura of dream-like self-reflection' (144). However, there is an important difference between the fantasy afforded by cinema and that realised through dance. As McRobbie explains,

> cinema offers a one-way fantasy which is directed solely through the gaze of the spectator towards the screen, the fantasy of dancing is more social, more reciprocated. This is because it allows simultaneously a dramatic display of the self and the body, with an equally dramatic negation of the self and the body. (144)

122

A second series of objections comes from Gary Clarke (1981/1990). He rejects the 'dichotomy between subcultures and . . . the rest of society as being straight, incorporated in a consensus, and willing to scream undividedly loud in any moral panic' (1990: 84). He also objects to the London-centredness of much subcultural theory and its suggestion that the appearance of a given youth subculture in the provinces is a telling sign of the subculture's incorporation (86). At the centre of Clarke's critique is a suspicion of the presence of an implicit cultural elitism structuring much subcultural theory.

> I would argue generally that the subcultural literature's focus on the stylistic deviance of a few contains (albeit implicitly) a similar treatment of the rest of the working class as unproblematically incorporated. This is evident, for example, in the distaste felt for youth deemed as outside subcultural activity – even though most 'straight' working-class youths enjoy the same music, styles, and activities as the subcultures – and in the disdain for such cults as glam, disco, and the ted revival, which lack 'authenticity'. Indeed, there seems to be an underlying contempt for 'mass culture' (which stimulates the interest in those who deviate from it) which stems from the work of the Marxism of the Frankfurt School and, within the English tradition, to the fear of mass culture expressed in *The Uses of Literacy*. (90)

If subcultural consumption is to remain an area of concern in cultural studies, Clarke suggests that future analysis 'should take the breakthrough of a style as its starting point' (92). Better still, cultural studies should focus on 'the activities of all youths to locate continuities and discontinuities in culture and social relations and to discover the meaning these activities have for the youths themselves' (95).

FAN CULTURE

Fans are the most visible part of the audience for popular cultural texts and practices. In recent years, fandom has come increasingly under the critical gaze of cultural studies. Traditionally, fans have been treated in one of two ways – ridiculed or pathologised. According to Joli Jenson (1992), 'The literature on fandom is

123

haunted by images of deviance. The fan is consistently characterized (referencing the term's origins) as a potential fanatic. This means that fandom is seen as excessive, bordering on deranged, behaviour' (9). Jenson suggests two typical types of fan pathology, 'the obsessed individual' (usually male) and 'the hysterical crowd' (usually female). She contends that both figures result from a particular reading and 'unacknowledged critique of modernity' in which fans are viewed 'as a psychological symptom of a presumed social dysfunction' (9). Fans are presented as one of the dangerous 'others' of modern life. 'We' are sane and respectable; 'they' are obsessed or hysterical.

Fans are conceived as the passive and pathological victims of the mass media. Whereas 'you' and 'I' can discriminate and create distance between ourselves and the objects of our pleasure (and thus stay 'normal'), fans cannot. The most common stereotypes are groups of hysterical girls and women who scream at the celebrities that lonely and obsessive boys and men dream of killing. Cultural studies does not seek to deny the reality of, say, Beatlemania, or the fact that Mark Chapman killed ex-Beatle John Lennon. But what it does deny is that this is the complete story (the only reality) of fandom. According to Jenson, both stereotypes tell us more about the influence of a dominant school of social thinking than they do about fandom.

> What is assumed to be true of fans – that they are potentially deviant, as loners or as members of a mob – can be connected with deeper, and more diffuse, assumptions about modern life. Each type mobilizes related assumptions about modern individuals: the obsessed loner invokes the image of the alienated 'mass man'; the frenzied crowd member invokes the image of the vulnerable, irrational victim of mass persuasion. (14)

In other words, fandom is a visible (pathological) symptom of the supposed cultural, moral and social decline which has inevitably followed the transition from rural and agricultural to industrial and urban society. At its most benign, fandom represents a desperate attempt to compensate for the shortcomings of modern life. Cultural studies was born in part out of a rejection of this kind of nostalgic and romantic way of thinking (see Storey 1993: 20–41).

124

Moreover, like the general discourse of which it forms a part, this is a discourse on other people. Fandom is what 'other people' do; 'we' always pursue interests, exhibit tastes and preferences. 'Furthermore', as Jenson points out, 'what "they" do is deviant, and therefore dangerous, while what "we" do is normal, and therefore safe' (19). Similarly, like the general discourse, it seeks to secure and police distinctions between class cultures. This is clear in the way in which fandom is assigned to the cultural activities of popular audiences, while dominant groups are said to have cultural interests, tastes and preferences. This is confirmed by the object(s) of admiration. Official or dominant culture produces aesthetic appreciation; fandom is only appropriate for the texts and practices of popular culture.[1] Moreover, distinction is established not just by the object of admiration but also in how the object is said to be admired. Popular audiences are said to display their pleasure to emotional excess, whereas the audiences for official or dominant culture are always able to maintain respectable aesthetic distance and control.

Perhaps the most interesting recent account of fan culture from within cultural studies is Henry Jenkins's *Textual Poachers* (1992). In an ethnographic investigation of a fan community (mostly, but not exclusively, white middle-class women), Jenkins approaches fandom as '*both* ... an academic (who has access to certain theories of popular culture, certain bodies of critical and ethnographic literature) and as a fan (who has access to the particular knowledge and traditions of that community)' (5). The study is written, as Jenkins is quick to point out, 'in active dialogue with the fan community':

> My practice from the outset has been to share each chapter with all of the quoted fans and to encourage their criticism of its contents. I have received numerous letters from fans, offering their own insights into the issues raised here and I have learned much from their reactions. I have met with groups of fans in open discussions of the text and have incorporated their suggestions into its revision. In some cases, I have inserted their reactions into the text, yet, even where this has not occurred

directly and explicitly, it must be understood that this text exists in active dialogue with the fan community. (7)

Jenkins's commitment to active dialogue is in part born out of his determination to use his 'institutional authority' to enable him to redefine 'the public identity of fandom', to challenge the negative stereotypes of fans as figures of ridicule or concern, 'and to encourage a greater awareness of the richness of fan culture' (9). The study is written to increase academic knowledge of fan culture, but also with an insistence that academics 'can learn *from* fan culture' (8).

Jenkins's principal theoretical source is the French cultural theorist Michel de Certeau (1984), who unpacks the term 'consumer' to reveal the activity which lies within the act of consumption: what he calls 'secondary production'. Consumption 'is devious, it is dispersed, but it insinuates itself everywhere, silently and almost invisibly, because it does not manifest itself through its own products, but rather through its *ways of using* the products imposed by a dominant economic order' (xii–xiii). For de Certeau, the cultural field is a site of continual conflict (silent and almost invisible) between the 'strategy' of cultural imposition (production) and the 'tactics' of cultural use (consumption). The cultural critic must be alert to 'the difference or similarity between . . . production . . . and . . . secondary production hidden in the process of . . . utilization' (xiii). He thus characterises the active consumption of texts as 'poaching': 'readers are travellers; they move across lands belonging to someone else, like nomads poaching their way across the fields they did not write' (174). The acts of reader appropriation are always in potential conflict with the 'scriptural economy' of textual producers and those institutional voices (professional critics, academics, etc.) who work, through an insistence on the authority of authorial/textual meaning, to limit and confine the productive proliferation and circulation of 'unauthorised' meanings. De Certeau's notion of 'poaching' is a rejection of this traditional model of reading, in which the purpose of reading is the passive reception of authorial/textual intent. It is a model in which reading is reduced to a question of being right or wrong. According to Jenkins,

> What is significant about fans in relation to de Certeau's model is that they constitute a particularly active and vocal community of consumers whose activities direct attention onto this process of cultural appropriation. . . . Fans are not unique in their status as textual poachers, yet, they have developed poaching to an art form. (127)

Jenkins differs from de Certeau in that he contends that unlike popular reading, which Jenkins characterises as 'transient meaning-production' (45), fan reading has an ongoing existence in discussions with other fan readers.

> Such discussions expand the experience of the text beyond its initial consumption. The produced meanings are thus more fully integrated into the readers' lives and are of a fundamentally different character from meanings generated through a casual and fleeting encounter with an otherwise unremarkable (and unremarked upon) text. For the fan, these previously 'poached' meanings provide a foundation for future encounters with the fiction, shaping how it will be perceived, defining how it will be used. (45)

A second difference between de Certeau's popular reader and the activities of fandom is that in fandom there is no hard distinction between readers and writers. Fan culture is a culture of both consumption and production. Fandom is not just about consumption, it is also about the production of texts – songs, poems, novels, fanzines, videos, etc. – made in response to the professional media texts of fandom.

According to Jenkins, there are three key features which mark fan culture's mode of appropriation of media texts: '[the] ways fans draw texts close to the realm of their lived experience; the role played by rereading within fan culture; and the process by which program information gets inserted into ongoing social interactions' (53).

First of all, then, fan reading is characterised by an intensity of intellectual and emotional involvement.

> The text is drawn close not so that the fan can be possessed by it but rather so that the fan may more fully possess it. Only by

> integrating media content back into their everyday lives, only by close engagement with its meanings and materials, can fans only consume the fiction and make it an active resource. (62)

Arguing against textual determinism (the text determines how it will be read and in so doing positions the reader in a particular ideological discourse; see chapter 3 above), Jenkins insists: 'The reader is drawn not into the preconstituted world of the fiction but rather into a world she [sic] has created from textual materials. Here, the reader's pre-established values are at least as important as those preferred by the narrative system' (63). Again, the difference between fan reader and other readers is a question of the intensity of intellectual and emotional involvement which constitute 'the reader's pre-established values'. The ordinary reader reads in a context of shifting interests; the fan reads from within the realms of the 'lived experience' of fandom.

Second, fans do not just read texts, they continually reread them. This profoundly changes the nature of the text–reader relationship. Roland Barthes (1975) contends that the rereading of texts alters a reader's experience of a text. Rereading undermines the operations of the 'hermeneutic code' (the ways in which a text poses questions to generate the desire to keep reading). Rereading thus shifts the reader's attention from 'what will happen' to 'how things happen', to questions of character relations, narrative themes, the production of social knowledges and discourses.

Finally, whereas most reading is a solitary process, performed in private, fans consume texts as part of a community. Fan culture is about the public display and circulation of meaning production and reading practices. Fans make meanings to communicate with other fans. Without the public display and circulation of these meanings, fandom would not be fandom.

> Organised fandom is, perhaps first and foremost, an institution of theory and criticism, a semistructured space where competing interpretations and evaluations of common texts are proposed, debated, and negotiated and where readers speculate about the nature of the mass media and their own relationship to it. (86)

As stated already, fan communities are not just bodies of enthusiastic readers. Fan culture is also about cultural production. Jenkins (1992: 162–77), for example, notes ten ways in which fans rewrite their favourite television shows. (1) *Recontextualisation*: the production of vignettes, short stories and novels which seek to fill in the gaps in broadcast narratives and suggest additional explanations for particular actions. (2) *Expanding the Series Timeline*: the production of vignettes, short stores and novels which provide background history of characters, etc. not explored in broadcast narratives, or suggestions for future developments beyond the period covered by the broadcast narrative. (3) *Refocalisation*: this occurs when fan writers move the focus of attention from the main protagonists to secondary figures. For example, female or black characters are taken from the margins of a text and given centre stage. (4) *Moral Realignment*: a version of refocalisation in which the moral order of the broadcast narrative is inverted (the villains become the good guys). In some versions, the moral order remains the same but the story is now told from the point of view of the villains. (5) *Genre Shifting*: characters from broadcast science-fiction narratives, say, are relocated in the realms of romance or the Western, for example. (6) *Crossovers*: characters from one television programme are introduced into another. For example, characters from *Dr Who* may appear in the same narrative as characters from *Star Wars*. (7) *Character Dislocation*: characters are relocated in new narrative situations, with new names and new identities. (8) *Personalisation*: the insertion of the writer into a version of their favourite television programme. For example, I could write a short story in which I am recruited by Dr Who to travel with him on the TARDIS on a mission to explore what has become of cultural studies in the twenty-fourth century. As Jenkins (171–2) points out, this subgenre of fan writing is discouraged by many in the fan community. (9) *Emotional Intensification*: the production of what are called 'hurt-comfort' stories in which favourite characters, for example, experience emotional crises. (10) *Eroticisation*: stories which explore the erotic side of a character's life. Perhaps the best-known of this subgenre of fan writing is 'slash' fiction, so called because it depicts same-sex relationships (as in Kirk/Spock, Bodie/Doyle, etc.).

In addition to fan fiction, fans make music videos in which images from favourite programmes are edited into new sequences to a soundtrack provided by a popular song; they make fan art; they produce fanzines; they engage in 'filking' (the writing and performing at conferences of songs – filk songs – about programmes, characters or fandom itself); and they organise campaigns (often with some success: see Jenkins 1992, especially chapter 4) to press television networks to bring back favourite programmes or to make changes in existing ones. As Jenkins points out, 'Fans are poachers who get to keep what they take and use their plundered goods as the foundations for the construction of an alternative cultural community' (223).

In his discussion of filking, Jenkins draws attention to a common opposition within filk songs between fandom and 'Mundania' (the world in which non-fans – 'mundane readers' or 'mundanes' – live). The difference between the two worlds is not simply one of intensity of response; 'they are also contrasted in terms of the shallowness and short-sightedness of mundane thinking' (264). 'Fans are defined in opposition to the values and norms of everyday life, as people who live more richly, feel more intensely, play more freely, and think more deeply than "mundanes" ' (268). According to Jenkins, 'Fandom constitutes . . . a space . . . defined by its refusal of mundane values and practices, its celebration of deeply held emotions and passionately embraced pleasures. Fandom's very existence represents a critique of conventional forms of consumer culture' (283).

What Jenkins finds particularly empowering about fandom is its struggle to create 'a more participatory culture' from 'the very forces that transform many Americans into spectators' (284).

> I am not claiming that there is anything particularly empowering about the texts fans embrace. I am, however, claiming that there is something empowering about what fans do with those texts in the process of assimilating them to the particulars of their lives. Fandom celebrates not exceptional texts but rather exceptional readings (though its interpretive practices make it impossible to maintain a clear or precise distinction between the two). (284)

Like the CCCS's model of subcultural reading, Jenkins's community of fandom struggles to resist the demands of the ordinary and the everyday. Whereas youth subcultures define themselves against parent and dominant cultures, the community of fandom sets itself in opposition to the everyday cultural passivities of 'Mundania'.

Lawrence Grossberg (1992b) is critical of the 'subcultural' model of fandom, in which 'fans constitute an elite fraction of the larger audience of passive consumers' (52).

> Thus, the fan is always in constant conflict, not only with the various structures of power, but also with the vast audience of media consumers. But such an elitist view of fandom does little to illuminate the complex relations that exist between forms of popular culture and their audiences. While we may all agree that there is a difference between the fan and the consumer, we are unlikely to understand the difference if we simply celebrate the former category and dismiss the latter one. (52)

Jenkins's own 'vanguardism' comes, at times, close to this model. Perhaps Fiske (1992b: 46) is right in his assertion that the real difference between a fan and an 'ordinary' reader is 'excess' – the fan is an excessive reader of popular culture.

SHOPPING AS POPULAR CULTURE

Going shopping is a complex activity. We may visit a shopping centre for a range of different, often contradictory, reasons. We may go to purchase a special gift or to buy the weekly groceries. We may go to look or to be looked at. Shopping centres, as Meaghan Morris (1988) points out, are used by different groups differently:

> there are different practices of use in one centre on any one day: some people may be there for the one and only time in their lives; there are occasional users choosing that centre rather than this on that day for particular, or quite arbitrary reasons; people may shop at one centre and go to another to socialize or hang around. The use of centres as meeting places (and sometimes for free warmth and shelter) by young people, pensioners, the unemployed and the homeless is a familiar part of their social function – often planned for, now, by centre

131

management (distribution of benches, video games, security guards). (200)

Consumption is always more than an economic activity – the consuming of products/the use of commodities to satisfy material needs. Consumption is also about dreams and desires, identities and communication. In Britain and the USA, behind watching television, shopping is the most popular leisure activity. In short, shopping has become popular culture.[2]

John Fiske describes shopping centres as 'cathedrals of consumption' (1989b: 13). It is a phrase he immediately regrets, given that it equates consumerism with rituals of profane worship.[3] Fiske is surely right to reject religion as a metaphor for the 'truth' of consumption. Shopping is not a passive ritual of subjugation to the power of consumerism. The truth of consumption is made and remade in the actual act(s) of shopping. Michael Schudson (1984) estimates that in the USA, 90 per cent of new products fall to attract enough consumers to remain in the marketplace. In Australia, John Sinclair (1987) estimates the figure to be about 80 per cent. This is more or less the same failure rate claimed by Simon Firth (1983) with regard to albums and singles in the UK and the USA (see chapter 6 above). As Fiske points out, 'The power of consumer discrimination evidenced here has no equivalent in the congregation: no religion could tolerate a rejection rate of 80 or 90 per cent of what it has to offer' (1989b: 14).

Bill Pressdee's (1986) research on the way in which unemployed youths in the South Australian town of Elizabeth use the local shopping centre points to further complexities of consumption. Shopping for the young people of Elizabeth means congregating at the local shopping centre not to buy what is on sale but to consume the public space of the mall. Pressdee invents the term 'proletarian shopping' to describe this practice. Young people are not alone in engaging in similar forms of shopping. They are frequently joined by tourists, escapees from bad weather, window shoppers and others who avail themselves of the facilities without necessarily contributing to the profit made by the shopping centre. Fiske (1989b: 18) cites a boutique-owner in an Australian shopping centre who estimated that for every thirty people who visited her shop, only one made a purchase.

Paul Willis (1990) argues that everyday cultural consumption operates by a process which he calls 'grounded aesthetics'.

> This is the creative element in a process whereby meanings are attributed to symbols and practices and where symbols and practices are selected, reselected, highlighted and recomposed to resonate further appropriate and particularized meanings. Such dynamics are emotional as well as cognitive. There are as many aesthetics as there are grounds for them to operate in. Grounded aesthetics are the yeast of common culture. (21)

Grounded aesthetics is the process through which ordinary people make cultural sense of the world: 'the ways in which the received natural and social world is made human to *them* and made, to however small a degree (even if finally symbolic), controllable by them' (22). Grounded aesthetic value is never intrinsic to a text or practice, a universal quality of its form; it is always generated in the 'sensuous/emotive/cognitive' act of consumption (how the text or practice is appropriated and 'used') (24). This is an argument against those who locate creativity only in the act of production – consumption being merely the recognition or misrecognition of the intentions of production. Against this, Willis insists on consumption as a symbolic act of creativity. Willis's 'fundamental point . . . is that "messages" are not now so much "sent" and "received" as *made* in reception. . . . "Sent message" communication is being replaced by "made message" communication' (135). A text or practice that may be judged to be intrinsically banal and uninteresting may, on the basis of its *production in use* within specific relations of consumption, be judged to be of great cultural interest and originality.

> People bring living identities to commerce and the consumption of cultural commodities as well as being formed there. They bring experiences, feelings, social position and social memberships to their encounter with commerce. Hence they bring a necessary creative symbolic pressure, not only to make sense of cultural commodities, but partly through them also to

133

> make sense of contradiction and structure as they experience them in school, college, production, neighbourhood, and as members of certain genders, races, classes and ages. The results of this necessary symbolic work may be quite different from anything initially coded into cultural commodities. (21)

Willis contends that the capitalist drive for profit produces contradictions which the symbolic creativity of the realm of common culture can exploit. But more than this, and more important than this, the capitalist drive for profit produces the very conditions for the production of the realm of common culture.

> No other agency has recognized this realm or supplied it with usable symbolic materials. And commercial entrepreneurship of the cultural field has discovered something real. For whatever self-serving reasons it was accomplished, we believe that this is an historical *recognition*. It counts and is irreversible. Commercial cultural forms have helped to produce an historical present from which we cannot now escape and in which there are many more materials – no matter what we think of them – available for necessary symbolic work than ever there were in the past. Out of these come forms not dreamt of in the commercial imagination and certainly not in the official one – forms which make up common culture. (19)

Willis agrees with Lovell's claim (see chapter 6 above) that capitalism is not a monolithic system. For example, while one capitalist bemoans the activities of the latest subculture, another embraces it with economic enthusiasm. It is these contradictions in the capitalist market system which have produced the realm of common culture.

> Commerce and consumerism have helped to release a profane explosion of everyday symbolic life and activity. The genie of common culture is out of the bottle – let out by commercial carelessness. Not stuffing it back in, but seeing what wishes may be granted, should be the stuff of our imagination. (27)

This entails the suggestion of 'the possibility of cultural emancipation working, at least in part, through ordinary, hitherto uncongenial economic mechanisms' (131). He sees the 'market', in part because of its contradictions – 'supplying materials for its own critique' (139) – and despite its intentions and its distortions, as enabling the symbolic creativity of the realm of common culture.

> People find on the market incentives and possibilities not simply for their own confinement but also for their own development and growth. Though turned inside out, alienated and working through exploitation at every turn, these incentives and possibilities promise more than any visible alternative. . . . Nor will it suffice any longer in the face of grounded aesthetics to say that modern 'consumer identities' simply repeat 'inscribed positions' within market-provided texts and artefacts. Of course the market does not provide cultural empowerment in anything like a full sense. There are choices, but not choices over choices – the power to set the cultural agenda. Nevertheless the market offers a contradictory empowerment which has not been offered elsewhere. It may not be the best way to cultural emancipation for the majority, but *it may open up the way to a better way* [my italics]. (160)

Perhaps Willis is too optimistic. But what is certain is that there is no simple politics of consumption. As Erica Carter (1984) points out, 'Passive manipulation or active appropriation, escapist delusion or Utopian fantasy, consumerism can be all or none of these' (191). Moreover, as Janice Radway (1992) contends, we should 'begin to understand that the conceptual opposition between consumption and criticism is itself a historically contingent construction that conceals the fact that all consumption involves criticism and that all criticism is itself wholly dependent on previous consumption' (515).

NOTES

1. Jenson (1992: 19–20) argues convincingly that it is possible to be a fan of James Joyce in much the same way as it is possible to be a fan of Barry Manilow.

2. Shopping centres are about so much more than buying things. Take the example of my local shopping centre, the MetroCentre, Gateshead. It is an attraction in its own right, attracting tourists from around Britain to its shops, cinema, bowling alley, restaurants and fairground. Meaghan Morris (1988) gives the example of Indooroopilly Shoppingtown in Queensland, Australia, as 'a place with a postcard' (209).

3. My local shopping centre, Gateshead's MetroCentre, may be a special case: it has its own full-time priest.

BIBLIOGRAPHY

Adorno, T. W. (1991) *The Culture Industry: Selected Essays on Mass Culture*, London: Routledge.

Adorno, T. W. (1994) 'On Popular Music', in J. Storey (ed.) (1994).

Allen, R. (ed.) (1992) *Channels of Discourse, Reassembled*, London: Routledge.

Althusser, L. (1969) *For Marx*, Harmondsworth: Penguin.

Althusser, L. (1971) *Lenin and Philosophy and Other Essays*, London: New Left Books.

Althusser, L. and Balibar, E. (1970) *Reading Capital*, London: New Left Books.

Ang, I. (1985) *Watching Dallas*, London: Methuen.

Ang, I. (1989) 'Wanted: Audience', in E. Selter et al. (eds) (1989).

Ang, I. (1990) *Desperately Seeking the Audience*, London: Routledge.

Ang, I. (1991) *Watching Television*, London: Routledge.

Ang, I. (1995) *Living Room Wars*, London: Routledge.

Ashley, B. (ed.) (1989) *The Study of Popular Fiction*, London: Pinter.

Barker, M. and Beezer, A. (eds) (1992) *Reading into Cultural Studies*, London: Routledge.

Barthes, R. (1967) *Elements of Sociology*, London: Jonathan Cape.

Barthes, R. (1973) *Mythologies*, London: Jonathan Cape.

Barthes, R. (1975) *The Pleasure of the Text*, New York: Hill and Wang.

Barthes, R. (1977) *Image – Music – Text*, London: Routledge.

Bennett, T. (ed.) (1990) *Popular Fiction*, London: Routledge.

Bennett, T. and Woollacott, J. (1987) *Bond and Beyond*, London: Macmillan.

137

Bennett, T. et al. (eds) (1981) *Culture, Ideology and Social Process*, London: Batsford Academic.

Bennett, T. et al. (eds) (1986) *Popular Culture and Social Relations*, Milton Keynes: Open University Press.

Bocock, R. and Thompson, K. (eds) (1992) *Social and Cultural Forms of Modernity*, Cambridge: Polity Press.

Bourdieu, P. (1984) *Distinction*, Cambridge, MA: Harvard University Press.

Bourdieu, P. (1993) *The Field of Cultural Production*, Cambridge: Polity Press.

Brantlinger, P. (1990) *Crusoe's Footsteps: Cultural Studies in Britain and America*, New York: Routledge.

Brooks, P. (1976) *The Melodramatic Imagination*, New Haven: Yale University Press.

Brunsdon, C. (1991) 'Pedagogies of the Feminine: Feminist Teaching and Women's Genres', *Screen* 32:4. Also in J. Storey (ed.) (1994).

Carter, E. (1984) 'Alice in the Consumer Wonderland: West German Case Studies in Gender and Consumer Culture', in A. McRobbie and M. Nava (eds) (1984).

Centre for Contemporary Cultural Studies (1982) *The Empire Strikes Back*, London: Hutchinson.

Certeau, M. de (1984) *The Practice of Everyday Life*, Berkeley: University of California Press.

Chambers, I. (1985) *Urban Rhythms: Pop Music and Popular Culture*, London: Macmillan.

Chambers, I. (1986) *Popular Culture: The Metropolitan Experience*, New York: Methuen.

Chodorow, N. (1978) *The Reproduction of Mothering*, Berkeley: University of California Press.

Clarke, G. (1990) 'Defending Ski-jumpers: A Critique of Theories of Youth Subcultures', in S. Frith and A. Goodwin (eds) (1990).

Clarke, J. et al. (1976) 'Subcultures, Culture and Class', in S. Hall and T. Jefferson (eds) (1976).

Cohen, P. (1980) 'Subcultural Conflict and Working-class Community', in S. Hall et al. (eds) (1980).

Collins, J. (1989) *Uncommon Cultures: Popular Culture and Post-modernism*, London: Routledge.

Connell, I. (1992) 'Personalities in the Popular Media', in P. Dahlgren and C. Sparks (eds) (1992).

Coward, R. (1984) *Female Desire*, London: Paladin.

Cruz, J. and Lewis, J. (eds) (1994) *Viewing, Reading, Listening*, Boulder: Westview Press.

Curran, J. and Gurevitch, M. (eds) (1991) *Mass Media and Society*, London: Edward Arnold.

Curti, L. (1992) 'What is Real and What is Not: Female Fabulations in Cultural Analysis', in L. Grossberg et al. (eds) (1992).

Dahlgren, P. (1992) 'Introduction', in P. Dahlgren and C. Sparks (eds) (1992).

Dahlgren, P. and Sparks, C. (eds) (1992) *Journalism and Popular Culture*, London: Sage.

Day, G. (ed.) (1990) *Readings in Popular Culture*, London: Macmillan.

Denselow, R. (1989) *When the Music's Over: The Story of Political Pop*, London: Faber and Faber.

Derrida, J. (1973) *Speech and Phenomena*, Evanston: North Western University Press.

Derrida, J. (1976) *Of Grammatology*, Baltimore: Johns Hopkins University Press.

Derrida, J. (1978) *Writing and Difference*, London: Routledge & Kegan Paul.

Docker, J. (1994) *Postmodernism and Popular Culture: A Cultural History*, Cambridge: Cambridge University Press.

During, S. (ed.) (1993) *The Cultural Studies Reader*, London: Routledge.

Dyer, R. (1977) 'Victim: Hermeneutic Project', *Film Form* 1: 2.

Dyer, R. (1981) 'Entertainment and Utopia', in R. Altman (ed.) *Genre: The Musical: A Reader*, London: Routledge & Kegan Paul.

Eagleton, T. (1983) *Literary Theory: An Introduction*, Oxford: Blackwell.

Easthope, A. (1991) *Literary into Cultural Studies*, London: Routledge.

Easthope, A. and McGowan, K. (eds) (1992) *A Critical and Cultural Theory Reader*, Milton Keynes: Open University Press.

Featherstone, M. (1991) *Consumer Culture and Postmodernism*, London: Sage.

Fiske, J. (1987) *Television Culture*, New York: Routledge.

Fiske, J. (1989a) *Understanding Popular Culture*, Boston, MA: Unwin Hyman.

Fiske, J. (1989b) *Reading Popular Culture*, Boston, MA: Unwin Hyman.

Fiske, J. (1992a) 'Popularity and the Politics of Information', in P. Dahlgren and C. Sparks (eds) (1992).

Fiske, J. (1992b) 'The Cultural Economy of Fandom', in L. Lewis (ed.) (1992).

Fiske, J. (1993) *Power Plays, Power Works*, London: Verso.

Fiske, J. (1994) *Media Matters*, Minneapolis: University of Minnesota Press.

Fiske, J. et al. (eds) (1987) *Myths of Oz: Reading Australian Popular Culture*, London: Allen & Unwin.

Frith, S. (1983) *Sound Effects*, London: Constable.

Frith, S. and Goodwin, A. (eds) (1990) *On Record: Rock, Pop and the Written Word*, New York: Pantheon.

Frith, S. and McRobbie, A. (1978) 'Rock and Sexuality', *Screen Education* 29.

Frow, J. and Morris, M. (1993) *Australian Cultural Studies: A Reader*, St Leonards: Allen & Unwin.

Gamman, L. and Marshment, M. (eds) (1988) *The Female Gaze: Women as Viewers of Popular Culture*, London: Verso.

Geraghty, C. (1991) *Women and Soap Opera*, Cambridge: Polity Press.

Gilroy, P. (1987) *There Ain't No Black in the Union Jack*, London: Hutchinson.

Gledhill, C. (1988) 'Pleasurable Negotiations', in E. U. Pribram (ed.) (1988).

Golding, P. and Murdock, G. (1991) 'Culture, Communications and Political Economy', in J. Curran and M. Gurevitch (eds) (1991).

Gramsci, A. (1971) *Selections from Prison Notebooks*, London: Lawrence and Wishart.

Gray, A. and McGuigan, J. (eds) (1993) *Studying Culture: An Introductory Reader*, London: Edward Arnold.

Gripsrud, J. (1992) 'The Aesthetics and Politics of Melodrama', in P. Dahlgren and C. Sparks (eds) (1992).

Grossberg, L. (1983) 'Cultural Studies Revisited', in M. Mander (ed.) *Communications in Transition*, New York: Praeger.

Grossberg, L. (1992a) *We Gotta Get Out of This Place*, London: Routledge.

Grossberg, L. (1992b) 'Is There a Fan in the House?: The Affective Sensibility of Fandom', in L. Lewis (ed.) (1992).

Grossberg, L. et al. (eds) (1992) *Cultural Studies*, London: Routledge.

Hall, S. (1980) 'Encoding and Decoding', in S. Hall et al. (eds) (1980).

Hall, S. (1981) 'Notes on Deconstructing "the Popular" ', in R. Samuel (ed.) (1981). Also in J. Storey (ed.) (1994).

Hall, S. (1985) 'The Rediscovery of Ideology: The Return of the Repressed in Media Studies', in V. Beechey and J. Donald (eds) *Subjectivity and Social Relations*, Milton Keynes: Open University Press.

Hall, S. (1992) 'Cultural Studies and its Theoretical Legacies', in L. Grossberg et al. (eds) (1992).

Hall, S. and Jefferson, T. (eds) (1976) *Resistance through Rituals*, London: Hutchinson.

Hall, S. and Whannel, P. (1964) *The Popular Arts*, London: Hutchison.

Hall, S. et al. (eds) (1980) *Culture, Media, Language*, London: Hutchinson.

Hebdige, D. (1976) 'The Meaning of Mod', in S. Hall and T. Jefferson (eds) (1976).

Hebdige, D. (1979) *Subculture: The Meaning of Style*, London: Routledge.

Hebdige, D. (1988) *Hiding in the Light*, London: Routledge.

Hoggart, R. (1990) *The Uses of Literacy*, Harmondsworth: Penguin.

Hollows, J. and Jancovich, M. (eds) (1995) *Approaches to Popular Film*, Manchester: Manchester University Press.

Jancovich, M. (1992) 'David Morley, The Nationwide Studies', in M. Barker and A. Beezer (eds) (1992).

Jenkins, H. (1992) *Textual Poachers*, New York: Routledge.

Jenson, J. (1992) 'Fandom as Pathology: The Consequences of Characterization', in L. Lewis (ed.) (1992).

Kellner, D. (1995) *Media Culture*, London and New York, Routledge.

Klein, M. (ed.) (1994) *An American Half Century: Postwar Culture and Politics in the USA*, London: Pluto.

Kubey, R. and Csikszentmihlyi, M. (1990) *Television and the Quality of Life*, Hillsdale: Lawrence Erlbaum Associates.

Lacan, J. (1977a) *The Four Fundamental Concepts of Psycho-Analysis*, London: Hogarth.

Lacan, J. (1977b) *Ecrits: A Selection*, London: Tavistock.

Leavis, F. R. (1930) *Mass Civilisation and Minority Culture*, Cambridge: Minority Press.

Leavis, F. R. and Thompson, D. (1977) *Culture and Environment*, Westport, CT: Greenwood Press.

Leavis, Q. D. (1978) *Fiction and the Reading Public*, London: Chatto & Windus.

Levi-Strauss, C. (1968) *Structural Anthropology*, New York: Basic Books.

Lewis, J. (1983) 'The Encoding/Decoding Model: Criticism and Redevelopments for Research on Decoding', *Media, Culture and Society 5*.

Lewis, L. (ed.) (1992) *The Adoring Audience: Fan Culture and Popular Media*, London: Routledge.

Longhurst, D. (ed.) (1989) *Gender, Genre and Narrative Pleasure*, London: Unwin Hyman.

Lovell, T. (1983) *Pictures of Reality*, London: British Film Institute.

MacCabe, C. (1974) 'Realism and the Cinema: Notes on some Brechtian Theses', *Screen* 15: 2.

Macherey, P. (1978) *A Theory of Literary Production*, London: Routledge & Kegan Paul.

McGuigan, J. (1992) *Cultural Populism*, London: Routledge.

McRobbie, A. (1980) 'Settling Accounts with Subcultures', *Screen Education* 34. Also in S. Frith and A. Goodwin (eds) (1990).

McRobbie, A. (1991) *Feminism and Youth Culture*, London: Macmillan.

McRobbie, A. (1992) 'Post-marxism and Cultural Studies: A Post-script', in L. Grossberg et al. (eds) (1992).

McRobbie, A. (1994) *Postmodernism and Popular Culture*, London: Routledge.

McRobbie, A. and Garber, J. (1976) 'Girls and Subcultures', in S. Hall and T. Jefferson (eds) (1976).

McRobbie, A. and Nava, M. (eds) (1984) *Gender and Generation*, London: Macmillan.

Marcuse, H. (1968) *One Dimensional Man*, London: Sphere.

Marris, P. and Thornham, S. (eds) (1995) *Media Studies: A Reader*, Edinburgh: Edinburgh University Press.

Marx, K. (1973) *Grundrisse*, Harmondsworth: Penguin.

Marx, K. (1975) *Early Writings*, Harmondsworth: Penguin.

Middleton, R. (1990) *Studying Popular Music*, Milton Keynes: Open University Press.

Milner, A. (1991) *Contemporary Cultural Studies*, Sydney: Allen & Unwin.

Modleski, T. (1982) *Loving with a Vengeance: Mass-produced Fantasies for Women*, Hamden, CT: Archon Books.

Moores, S. (1993) *Interpreting Audiences*, London: Sage.

Morley, D. (1980) *The 'Nationwide' Audience*, London: British Film Institute.

Morley, D. (1986) *Family Television*, London: Comedia.

Morley, D. and Chen, K.-H. (eds) (1995) *Stuart Hall: Critical Dialogues in Cultural Studies*, London: Routledge.

Morris, M. (1988) 'Things to Do with Shopping Centres', in S. Sheridan (ed.) (1988).

Mukerji, C. and Schudson, M. (eds) (1991) *Rethinking Popular Culture*, Berkeley: University of California Press.

Mulvey, L. (1975) 'Visual Pleasure and Narrative Cinema', *Screen* 16:3.

Nava, M. (1987) 'Consumarism and Its Contradictions', *Cultural Studies* 1: 2.

Open University (1982) *Popular Culture (U203)*, Milton Keynes: Open University Press.

Palmer, J. (1991) *Potboilers: Methods, Concepts and Case Studies in Popular Fiction*, London: Routledge.

Parkin, F. (1971) *Class Inequality and Political Order*, London: Paladin.

Pawling, C. (Ed.) (1984) *Popular Fiction and Social Change*, London: Macmillan.

Penley, C. (ed.) (1988) *Feminism and Film Theory*, New York: Routledge/British Film Institute.

Pressdee, B. (1986) 'Agony or Ecstasy: Broken Transitions and the New Social State of Working-class Youth in Australia', Occasional Papers, South Australia Centre for Youth Studies, South Australia College of Adult Education, Magill, South Australia.

Pribram, E. D. (ed.) (1988) *Female Spectators*, London: Verso.

Punter, D. (ed.) (1986) *Introduction to Contemporary Cultural Studies*, London: Longman.

Radway, J. (1987) *Reading the Romance*, London: Verso.

Radway, J. (1992) 'Mail-order Culture and Its Critics: The Book-of-the-Month Club, Commodification and Consumption, the Problem of Cultural Authority', in L. Grossberg et al. (eds) (1992).

Riesman, D. (1990) 'Listening to Popular Music', in S. Frith and A. Goodwin (eds) (1990).

Roman, L. G. et al. (eds) (1988) *Becoming Feminine: The Politics of Popular Culture*, London: Falmer Press.

Rosselson, L. (1979) 'Pop Music: Mobilizer or Opiate', in C. Gardner (ed.) *Media, Politics, Culture*, London: Macmillan.

Ryan, M. and Kellner, D. (1988) *Camera Politica*, Bloomington: Indiana University Press.

Samuel, R. (ed.) (1981), *People's History and Socialist Theory*, London: Routledge.

Sarup, M. (1993) *An Introductory Guide to Post-Structuralism and Postmodernism*, Hemel Hempstead: Harvester Wheatsheaf.

Saussure, F. de (1974) *Course in General Linguistics*, London: Fontana.

Schudson, M. (1984) *Advertising: The Uneasy Persuasion*, New York: Basic Books.

Seiter, E. et al. (eds) (1989) *Remote Control*, London: Routledge.

Sheridan, S. (ed.) (1988) *Grafts: Feminist Cultural Criticism*, London: Verso.

Shiach, M. (1989) *Discourse on Popular Culture*, Cambridge: Polity Press.

Sim, S. (ed.) (1995) *The A–Z Guide to Literary and Cultural Theorists*, Hemel Hempstead: Harvester Wheatsheaf.

Sinclair, J. (1987) *Images Incorporated*, London: Croom Helm.

Sparks, C. (1992) 'Popular Journalism: Theories and Practice', in P. Dahlgren and C. Sparks (eds) (1992).

Stacey, J. (1994) *Star Gazing: Hollywood and Female Spectatorship*, London: Routledge.

Storey, J. (1993) *An Introductory Guide to Cultural Theory and Popular Culture*, Hemel Hempstead: Harvester Wheatsheaf.

Storey, J. (ed.) (1994) *Cultural Theory and Popular Culture: A Reader*, Hemel Hempstead: Harvester Wheatsheaf.

Storey, J. (ed.) (1996) *What is Cultural Studies: A Reader*, London: Edward Arnold.

Storey, J. and Johnson, D. (1994) 'The Politics of Pop and the War in the Gulf', in J. Walsh (ed.) (1995).

Street, J. (1986) *Rebel Rock: The Politics of Popular Music*, Oxford: Oxford University Press.

Strinati, D. (1995), *An Introduction to Theories of Popular Culture*, London: Routledge.

Taylor, H. (1989) *Scarlett's Women*, London: Virago.

Taylor, L. (1995) 'From Psychoanalytic Feminism to Popular Feminism', in J. Hollows and M. Jancovich (eds) (1995).

Thwaites, T., Davis, L. and Mules, W. (1994) *Tools for Cultural Studies: An Introduction*, South Melbourne: Macmillan.

Traube, E. (1992) *Dreaming Identities: Class, Gender, and Generation in 1980s Hollywood Movies*, Boulder: Westview Press.

Turner, G. (1988) *Film as Social Practice*, London: Routledge.

Turner, G. (1990) *British Cultural Studies*, Boston, MA: Unwin Hyman.

Veblen, T. (1953) *A Theory of the Leisure Class*, New York: Mentor Books.

Volosinov, V. (1973) *Marxism and the Philosophy of Language*, London: Seminar Press.

Walsh, J. (ed.) (1995) *The Gulf War Did Not Happen*. Aldershot: Arena.

Weedon, C. (1987) *Feminist Practice and Poststructuralist Theory*, Oxford: Blackwell.

Williams, R. (1976) *Keywords*, London: Fontana.

Williamson, J. (1986) *Consuming Passions*, London: Marion Boyars.

Willis, P. (1978) *Profane Culture*, London: Routledge & Kegan Paul.

Willis, P. (1990) *Common Culture*, Milton Keynes: Open University Press.

Winship, J. (1987) *Inside Women's Magazines*, London: Pandora.

Wright, W. (1975) *Sixguns and Society*, Berkeley: University of California Press.

INDEX

145

Index

'myth', 88, 89, 90, 92
Mythologies, 87

'Nationwide' Audience, The, 14, 17
Nationwide, 13, 14, 16, 17
'negotiation', 67, 68, 79, 95, 96

Oedipus complex, 61, 63
'On Popular Music', 93–5

Parkin, F., 15
parole, 56, 92
Pecheux, M., 45
'people versus the 'power-bloc',
the', 77
'Photographic Message, The', 89
pleasure, 5, 6, 18, 21, 22, 23, 24, 26,
51, 65, 67, 78, 94, 101, 106, 107,
108, 125
political economy of culture, 95,
96, 98, 99
polysemy, 91
popular culture, 1, 2, 3, 5, 6, 7, 8,
20, 25, 26, 27, 67, 70, 75, 77, 87,
125, 131
popular fiction, 29–53
popular music, 93–112
pop music culture, 100, 101
popular press, 75–80
postmodernism, 5, 117
poststructuralism, 55, 60, 61, 65,
114–15
Presley, E., 104, 107
Pressdee, B., 132
'problematic the', 30, 33
Profane Culture, 103
production in use, 4, 5, 6, 103, 133
psychoanalysis, 61, 65, 67, 114–15

race, 2, 68, 69, 92
racism, 111
Radway, J., 47, 48, 49, 50, 51, 52
Raise the Titanic, 26
reading formation (s), 30, 43, 44, 45
Reading The Romance, 47
'relay', 91
Reagan, R., 109
Redding, O., 106
Reisman, D., 102
Resistance Through Rituals, 101
Rock Against Racism, 111

romance reading, 30, 47, 48, 49,
50, 51, 52
Rosselson, L., 96

Saussure, F. de, 55, 57, 60, 87
Schudson, M., 132
scriptural economy, 79, 126
semiology, 90
semiotic guerilla warfare, 26
'sent message communication', 133
Sex Pistols, 109
shopping as popular culture, 113,
131–35
signifier/signified, 55, 60, 63, 64,
87, 88, 90
Simmel, G., 116, 117
Sinclair, J., 132
Sixguns and Society, 54, 57
Smith, A., 30, 31
Sparks, C., 76, 78
spectatorship, 68, 69, 71, 73, 74
Stacey, J., 68, 69, 70, 71, 72, 74
'Stand By Your Man', 107
Star Wars, 129
Storey, J., 8
structuralism, 9, 54, 55, 56, 57,
61, 120
subcultures, 102, 103, 104, 113,
117–123, 130, 131
subject and subjectivity, 61, 62, 63
symbolic, the, 62, 63, 64, 115
symptomatic reading, 30, 31, 34

Taylor, L., 67
television, 9–27
Textual Poachers, 125
textual poaching, 126, 127, 130
Theory of Literary Production, A, 31
Theory of the Leisure Class, The, 116
Thompson, D., 29
to-be-looked-at-ness, 65

Ullman, T., 109
unconscious, 63
use value, 96, 97, 98
Uses of Literacy, The, 121, 123
utopian sensibility, 70

Veblen, T., 116, 117
Verne, J., 34
Vietnam War, 109, 110

147